LET YOUR LIGHT SHINE

Living in your Personal Power

JUDITH COATES

Books by the Author

BE WHO YOU BE

Enlightenment Series by J L Coates

SECOND CHANCES

Copyright@2012

Library and Archives Canada Cataloguing in Publication Judith Coates

ISBN-13: 978-0-9880735-1-7

ISB 10:0 9880735-1-X

Cover design – artist unknown- taken from internet

Printed in USA by Createspace

DEDICATION

To my family and friends who willingly accompanied me along my journey, and tolerated my strange ideas.

I couldn't have done this without you.

TABLE OF CONTENTS

ACKNOWLEDGEMENTS

Thank you to my Editor Dianne Tchir, and my Advisors and readers Clarice Nelson and Jennie England. I appreciate that you were able to point out where I was off track and argue with my ideas,

Thank you to the creator and artist of the cover picture. This is beautiful picture, which came over the internet, expresses exactly what I was trying to say and was perfect for my purpose. I would love to be able to acknowledge you and show my appreciation for your talent. No theft of your rights is intended.

Don't hide your light under a basket! Instead put it on a stand and let it shine for all.

You are the light of the world - like a city on a mountain glowing in the night for all to see.

Mathew 5: 14-15
Chicken Soup for the Soul Bible

PROLOGUE

Five years ago, when I began my journey, I was not the person I am today. Probably I look the same, maybe a little blonder, perhaps a pound or so heavier (ouch), but back then I had some bad habits that kept me frustrated and stuck. I didn't know who I was, or where I was going in my life. I didn't have a clue as to what I wanted. At that time I was asking myself *"is this all there is?"* I was approaching the age of seniority and didn't feel older or wiser. In fact I still don't. To me, age is just a random number.

Looking back I realized that I was a people pleaser, my spirit was exhausted trying to keep everybody happy, but inside I felt alone and frustrated. I was afraid of losing the rest of what I had in my life. I no longer had a job to get up and go to every morning. I was blaming my husband for selling our business out from under me. I had gone along with his idea, without considering what the ramifications would be.

After our mom passed away, my brother and I were rejected by our brothers and sisters. I was telling myself *"if my own brothers and sisters didn't want me, how could anybody else?"* A short time later my brother died an untimely death from cancer at the age of fifty six, leaving me alone to deal with their rejection. I had yet to face the fact that wanting to belong to my family was wishful thinking. Nothing I could say or do was going to change the situation.

When I look back, I see I could have used some professional help, but never considered that option at the time. I thought I was handling the circumstances rather well.

Inside I was crying out *"I want to be loved. I want to be a part of my family. I am a good person; I don't understand why this is happening."*

Somehow I lost me in the process of living. My goal of trying to keep everybody happy was based upon the belief that if I could accomplish that, they would want me. The more I tried, the bigger a failure I felt I was.

What I didn't understand at the time was that I was allowing myself to be taken for granted and bullied. Because I saw the attention as validation of who I was, I was fine with that. I have always had a problem saying "no" because I don't want to cause any dissension. Besides saying "yes" made me feel good.

My business life was a mess because that was where my insecurities were being manifested. It seemed that no matter what I did, I was left wanting. I always seemed to not measure up or accomplish what I set out to do. I felt like I was un-deserving and going nowhere fast. At the time I didn't know my destiny lay someplace else.

I first met my coach, Jennie England of Wisdom in Action, when I took a teleconference communication course. I thought that if I could learn to speak up, I would be more effective with the women I was working with. After two six week courses I approached her about individual coaching.

Something drew me to her. Perhaps it was because she was soft spoken, maybe because she wasn't judgmental. Whatever the reason, my inner voice was telling me that she offered exactly what I needed. I knew in my heart I had to continue working with her. This was one of those cases that when the pupil is ready, the teacher shows up.

In the beginning, our sessions were about my business and holding myself accountable, actually doing what I said I would do. Somehow this changed into her guiding me into finding and claiming my own power. I thank God for bringing her into my life.

Before I go any further, what do I mean by power? Other words for power are might, strength, or to do something in a particular way. Power means capitalizing on our strengths, not focusing on what we can't do, but on what we can.

I am truly amazed when I see where I am today, all of which came about as a result of my journey of trying find and recognize who I was inside; not the persona I presented to the world, but the person who felt lost, afraid and alone.

My first book *BE WHO YOU BE* was written because writing down what I was learning helped me understand. Writing has always come easy to me. God gives each of us a talent and this is the one he has given me. I don't remember where the idea of putting my thoughts into a book came from. I thought if I was battling demons, then others had to be too. I thought that if I shared what I was learning with others, then my learning and experiences may help them those in a similar situation.

As I began writing this second book I struggled with what direction to follow. Realizing that I wasn't the person I was, and that now my mind and thoughts are in a completely different place, made me want to share the rest of my journey.

This is merely a continuation of the process of one woman encouraging and showing the way to another, so that we may become the empowered person we are meant to be. Once again I am sharing my learning with you.

In my first book I wrote "God doesn't make "Nobody's," He only makes "Somebody's." You are a unique special individual. Become the person He wants to you to be. Become the light for another to follow. Step into your power. Although your life is a journey you must travel alone, there will be many companions who will travel part way with you.

In my own way I am offering you a few tips that worked for me and may assist you in some way. I sincerely hope they do. Even though I am offering you encouragement, I am still in the process of becoming. Come, take my hand, and we will learn together.

INTRODUCTION

I am writing this on a cold January morning before I go find my car under the heavy snowfall we received this weekend. I call these gray days because the white of the snow blends into the gray of the sky. Everything is the same degree of drabness.

I am working on my dining room table amid the clutter of papers, my journal, bills, my husband's lap top and other projects I am working on. Some of you might see this is as a mess, but to me, this is organized confusion.

Across the street, silhouetted against the gray sky is a large old Maple tree stretching its limbs fifty or more feet into the air. Each winter, this bare tree stands like a sentinel, guarding our street while it rests from the previous summer's glorious display.

As the days lengthen and become warmer, the tree awakens. First tiny buds appear, then the larger green leaves which provide shade and homes for the summer birds nesting among its branches.

The tree stands tall, bending and swaying in the gentle breezes. During the summer storms it stands fast, withstanding the driving rain and powerful winds.

As the days shorten and nights become cooler, the first frost changes the leaves from green to a brilliant display of red, yellow, and orange. On a quiet evening I can hear the leaves falling and landing on the pavement. Our street becomes a brilliant carpet of colour until the wind sends the leaves skittering down the road. When the last leaf has fallen, the tree once again rests until the time comes to repeat its cycle of life. During the winter, the frost fairies come out to paint the still branches with sparkling diamonds which shimmer when the sun kisses them.

To me, this tree symbolizes what life is about. Each year the tree grows, blooms, and then rests waiting for the opportunity to begin again.

Our lives are like that. We face a problem, deal with what we must, and find a solution which brings it to an end. This prepares us for the next phase of our life because we learn and grow from the experience.

Once again, I look at the tree. The biggest and heaviest branches are located at the bottom, the next grow a fraction smaller than the one before. This is nature's way of insuring the tree doesn't become top heavy and topple over. Its base is firmly rooted in the ground, just as we are rooted by our faith and the values we use to govern our lives.

From each branch smaller branches grow, which in turn produce smaller branches until they are barely visible against the gray sky. These branches symbolize the paths of our difficulties with the understanding that "these too shall end."

Today a bird is playing in the bare branches, hopping from one to another. Other times, I watch two squirrels playing hide and seek or chasing each other up and down the thick tree trunk. The tree, the bird, the squirrels are all exactly as they should be, a part of the circle of life. In this instance each is serving the purpose they were created for. Sometimes, on these gray days, I wish I was that bird, able to fly free and leave my problems and insecurities behind.

I believe that each of us has been placed upon this earth for a reason. All of the trials and tribulations we face serve a purpose in developing the person we are to become. They serve to improve our effectiveness, strengthen and empower us.

My first book chronicles the personal learning and growth I gained while working with my Life Skills coach Jennie England. With her help, I learned to put my past behind me and put what was good for me first, and to step into my world and be the person I am meant to be.

Sometime after my book was completed, I realized that I hadn't yet moved on enough to complete the process. I was still needy at times, anxious, and fearful, easily slipping into my old habits and thinking. Why? Because I was still in my comfort zone and these actions had always served me well in my life until now.

I realized that I was actually saying *"do as I say, not do as I do."* My book offered advice and practical solutions for each of us to become more, and be more, but I wasn't following my own advice. If I was to complete the process of honouring myself as a person, I had to practice what I preached.

The question became, how do I take my new learning and put it into action? I realized that none of us can move forward when we have one foot stuck in the past and the other in the present. The past is our crutch, our reasons for where we are today and why we are content to stay there. Living in our comfort zone enables us to know what to expect and predict what the results of our actions will be. There are few, if any surprises.

One day my daughter said to me "mom, you are really good at starting, but not so good at finishing." *I started on this journey, worked hard, but like the bird on the branch, I was content to sit and look around. If I was going to complete the process of honouring who I was, then the time had come to take a leap of faith off my branch and see if I could fly.*

In order to learn from any process, we need to apply our new knowledge in a way that serves our purpose. We have to give ourselves permission to begin moving forward. To those of us who are fear ridden, and anxious, this is just plain scary. We allow our anxiety to take precedence and challenge our new truth. Our path is clearly marked in front of us, but we are reluctant to take the first step. We procrastinate. We feed our anxiety with more anxiety. We do everything possible so that we don't have to face up to our reality. We over think and search for answers to questions we may never be asked.

Every journey begins with a single step. Each activity involves getting started. The Tips I am sharing with you are the same ones I took on my journey to living a life without fear and anxiety. Sometimes I feel like giving up, and then I look at the tree and realize that we too need the winters of our life to rest and heal. When we are tired, lonely or afraid, we must take the necessary time to rest before beginning again. We are meant to live life to the fullest, always growing, always learning and enjoying our journey.

WHERE I AM FROM

I am the oldest of seven- four girls, three boys,
A mother who loved me but settled for what is,
A dad who worked hard, an ex-alcoholic
A man who valued family above all
because he never had one.

I am from singing lessons, violin lessons,
Explorers, the city.
I am a high school graduate,
Lab. & X-ray technician, Berwyn Hospital.

I am from careful accounting,
worrying about money, never having enough.
A mom who scrimped and did without,
a dad who only wanted the best.

I am from working hard in school, in training.
Accepting challenges and
never quitting.

I am a product of tears, despair,
from chemical imbalance
to loving life and being here.

I am a person of faith!
From Sunday school to choir practice
from United to Catholic.

I am a person
willing to give and
receive nothing in return.

I am from Calder, railway yards and
train rides to grandma's.
Motorcycle rides, wind blowing in my hair
Car rides with dad.
Gravel pits in the summer,
alone in the winter.

I love my husband and kids,
miss my parents and their home
rejected,
but willing to forgive.

I am from independence, security and achievement
never giving up.
I am from future dreams,
providing for my husband and kids.

I am from classrooms to board rooms
From Parent councils, School board
and Adult Learning.

I am from futility to fertility
and God given children.
I am from Mary Kay –
Go give, reaching for dreams.

I am from storytelling in the yellow chair,
family holidays, hockey games,
skipping ropes, figure skates
and basketball.

I am from UFA,
sharing and caring
striving, moving ahead

loving what I do,
ever changing days.

We are forged from our past, but share in our future.
Destined to realize whatever we choose
Let's go there together!
Let's laugh there together!
And be soulfully rich this moment too.

Written July 2002

TIP # 1

YOU ARE NOT ALONE

This morning I am sitting pen in hand staring at a blank sheet of paper. Well, it's not really blank, there are lines waiting to be filled with words of wisdom, but I don't know where to start. I pretend you are sitting beside me as if you are one of my children. You are hurting, feeling unappreciated, possibly overwhelmed and need someone to listen to you.

Although we cannot be together in this context, I offer you the same words of encouragement I would offer them. You have value and worth. You are here on this earth, today, for a reason. God has a plan for you. Every sorrow, every joy, every defeat and every victory are all a part of the Master's plan. Because of your experiences, you will be able to provide support to another soul in need. Your life has a purpose, and only you can fulfil that purpose.

I would tell you how unique and special you are. There will only ever be one of you. Nobody will have your gifts, your talents, your experiences, your eyes or your temperament. After God made you, he threw the mould away. You are an original!

Because there is only ever going to be one of you, it stands to reason that you are to love and care for this precious gift. No other person will be able to do this as well as you. You alone know what you need, what your hopes, your expectations and your dreams are.

I would try and convince you to think about yourself –

to find and develop your strengths, and do what is right for you. Only then will you fully impact those who love and depend upon you.

It is true that I can clothe you, feed and nurture you as I did when you were a baby. I can need you, provide for your physical wants and desires, but I cannot give you the self-esteem, self-confidence, self-reliance and self-love you require. That is an inside job that only you are capable of doing. I can travel alongside you in your journey to self-awareness, but I cannot take your trip for you.

I wish I could. I wish I could lift the burdens off your shoulders but I can't. Instead, I step back and try not to tell you what to do, or push you into doing what I think you should. Sometimes you cry out for me to take the pain away, but I realize that if I do, I will also be taking away your power.

As angry as you may become, and as much as it hurts me, I know the best thing is for you to go through your experience so you emerge on the other side feeling empowered. What you learn from your experience becomes part of what makes you unique. In giving this to you, I am also giving myself the power to look after me.

Of course, there will be times I will step in to relieve the burden from your shoulders. In doing so I am giving you time and space to grapple with your demons, determine a course of action, and gather the courage and strength you need to keep going.

Learning to love and accept ourselves is a process. There will be moments of break through and moments when we wonder if this is all worth the hassle. Nothing worthwhile comes easy. We have to work for what we want. Don't give up on yourself! You can and will, in time, get through whatever is going on in your life right now. Better days do lie ahead.

So, how do we learn about this process to self-awareness and becoming all that we are meant to be? First we need to realize that we aren't perfect and never will be. Although many like to pretend otherwise, nobody has a perfect life. We have all done and said things we don't want another soul to know about. In some ways, we have all been emotionally crippled or mentally scarred. We have had crushing defeats and momentous victories. We have climbed the highest mountain and reached the deepest depths of the ocean. In a split second our normal way of life has irrevocably been changed as we experience life and death.

Whether we realize it or not, much of this is out of our control. We are simply along for the ride hanging on with every fibre of our being. Yet, when our experience ends, we are often left with unanswered questions. *"What if I had done this or said that? I should have been able to see what was coming, why didn't I? Now what?"*

Each time we do this, take responsibility or blame for something that wasn't ours in the first place, we chip a little piece of ourselves away. During the times we should be our own best friend, we become our own worst enemy. We need to become our own biggest fan and number one cheer leader.

"Whoa, Stop?' we cry out, that goes against everything we have ever been taught. I don't know about you but I was told, "don't be so selfish. Nobody likes people who only think of themselves" and so on. We are conditioned, as children, to value others more than we value ourselves, I am asking you to put all of those teachings aside for a short period of time and learn to value who you are.

Only when we truly understand who we are, what we stand for, and what we have to offer can we share our unique gifts and talents. We are given the power to make a difference in the lives of others when we begin to look after our own spiritual, physical, emotional and mental needs first.

TIP #2

KNOW THY SELF

Before beginning the actual process of learning to honor who we are, we need to begin defining who we are, and what we believe in. We are not that brave happy face we put forward at work, nor the victim we sometimes portray. We are not the person our roles define us as, but neither have we taken the time to define who we really are. Who is the person deep inside, the one we often refuse to acknowledge?

Many of us go day to day functioning as we are expected to. We are on high blood pressure medication, anti-depressants, reading self-help books, desperately searching for that magic word or thought that is going to change our life. We continually look to outside forces, not recognizing or understanding that we already know the answers to our questions. We pray for guidance that never seems to come.

The searching, finding, recognizing and utilizing this information is a lifetime job. As soon as we think we have everything figured out we get slammed broadside, and end up having to redefine ourselves again.

I began my journey with the question *is this all there is? What do I want to do for the rest of my years? Why do I think as I do? Why do I do what I do? What goes on in my head most of the time?*

In search of an answer I get out my trusty old ragged dictionary out and looked up the word "self." To my surprise there were two pages of words that began with that word. Now what?

The definition of self is "one's own person," basically who we think we are? Some of the words were positive such as self-esteem, self-confidence and self-reliance. Others were self-loathing, selfish, self-conscious, and self-deprecating – you get the idea. As I read each word I could see how we think about ourselves either uplifts our spirit or drags us down.

Where do I start? I don't want to bore you with all of the definitions from my Funk and Wagnall, but I will mention a few:

SELF ESTEEM - how much or how little we think of ourselves? Thankfully this is not a permanent condition and can vary many times a day. The other day I got my hair cut. When I left the stylist shop I was feeling good about how my hair looked, and in less than five minutes I received three compliments.

The next morning I got up and scared myself when I looked in the mirror. My hair was askew, sticking up in places, flattened in others. Nothing had changed from the day before, but I didn't feel as good about myself. Gone was that confident air I had because I looked great. I was thinking more along the line of maybe I should shave it all off and buy a wig.

One thing we must try to realize is that when another person expresses something negative about us or to us, they are merely stating their opinion. This doesn't mean it's true. You know different, and what we think of ourselves is far more important than the useless prattle coming out of their mouths.

SELF CONFIDENCE - is a learned trait. When I first started in sales, I would get myself worked up to the point that I would be sick to my stomach before I left home. I will say though, that I was persistent.

Over time I learned to confidently stand up in front of a hundred people, and tell my story, teach or share something I had written. The more we do something, the better we become at doing it. First we develop confidence in one area, and this eventually spills over into the other areas of our life.

SELF Control - is about controlling one's own actions. This is a tough one, because when we are attacked, our first inclination is to retaliate. Sometimes though, what we don't do is more effective than what we want to do. The morning after my mom's funeral, I was sitting with my brothers and sisters as we were trying to decide what to do next. Out of the blue, my youngest sister verbally attacked me. I was stunned, in fact I was speechless (which doesn't happen very often.). I wanted to argue with her. No, what I really wanted to do was grab her and shake her and find out where all of this venom was coming from, but I said nothing. What was the point? What would I prove? All I would end up doing was making a bad situation worse, but it took everything I had to keep my mouth shut.

SELF PRESERVATION - is about looking after our heart as well as our head. This is choosing what to stand up for, when to walk away and how to protect ourselves in the process. There are times we feel completely beaten down and demoralized. We are stressed to the max. We have nothing left to give.

When we feel this way, the time has come to be gentle with ourselves, to feed our soul, to spend time taking care of our own needs. We don't always have to be strong. We have to learn to turn off the world and look after our mental, emotional, and spiritual needs.

In his book, *"Man's Search for Meaning,"* Victor Frankl, an eminent Psychiatrist, wrote of his time in Auschwitz concentration camp. He says "everything can be taken from a man but one thing, the last of the human freedoms, to choose our attitude in any given set of circumstances, to choose one's own way."

When you feel defeated, step back, and pretend you are observing your life, and then decide how much more of yourself you are willing to invest in this particular situation. Strive to see the bigger picture.

You may have to ask yourself has the time come to stop what you are doing or are you able to see another way? There does come a time when we have to admit we have been defeated, and walk away, trusting the situation will resolve as it's supposed to.

SELF RELIANCE - is the knowing that the only person who can give you what you need is YOU. Please note I'm not advocating "If I want it done I will do it myself" thinking. Many times our needs feel so deep we can't verbalize them. We have to find the way to help ourselves.

My first night in the Psychiatric ward terrified me. I was irrational with fear. *What if this doesn't help? How had I ended up in such a mess and a complete failure?*

Since I was a young child I have always had a deep faith. That night, the only way I could find any peace of mind was to get down on my knees and desperately pray for help. The answer I received was "I am here for you, but you are the only one who can help yourself." I began fighting back against the dark forces that threatened to overcome me. First I learned, and then began to understand that these simple words were to become the ray of sunshine and hope that would give me the strength to come out of a very dark place.

I learned, albeit slowly, to recognize when I have too much going on and am feeling overwhelmed. Basically I remove myself from the situation for a few hours. I get in my car, crank up the music, take myself for lunch, visit the book store or just wander around window shopping. In essence I feed my soul with peace, give myself a break and spend some much needed time on me. I call it running away from home. This brief interlude gives me whatever I need to get back to life and deal with the circumstances. Nothing has changed, but I looked after me first.

I have also come to realize that self-reliance is a matter of our own perception. Sometimes I have to stop and ask myself *"is this is true or is it the way I am looking at this particular problem. Am I really not capable of doing this or do I just think I need another to do it for me?"*

When my kids were small they had a habit of flushing things down the toilet- toys, trucks, dog bones, rubber balls, you name it. After paying for a plumber several times I decided I to learn how to fix this myself. I actually became very good at taking the toilet bowl off, turning it upside down in the tub, removing the offending object, and putting everything back together again.

In Jack Whyte's book "The Eagle" he calls perception a word of power. I quote "perception can govern how people behave, even how they live. Perception can cause people to change their ways and adapt new ideas and beliefs. Perception can change destinies."

If you think you are broken, you are. If you think you can make a contribution to this world you will. Self-reliance is daring to ask the hard questions about how and what you are thinking, and then trusting your own answers.

Our perception of our world is our reality. When we change our way of thinking or interpretation, our reality changes accordingly.

Although we need to practice self-reliance, we also need support and encouragement from the people around us. Their varying opinions help alter our perceptions and our world.

Although these people can be very influential in our life, YOU are the only one you can depend on. You already have everything you need to answer your questions; all you need to do is trust the answers you receive.

My dictionary had other words such as self-defeating, self-loathing, self-deprecation, self-incrimination. Once again, our thinking comes from our perception. To make changes in our lives we first need to examine our thoughts, and then adapt them as necessary.

I believe that most people carry inside them the seeds of good. Instead of always being the first to put ourselves down, we need to look for the good within us, and find the gifts or talents we have to offer to the world.

We need to watch our self-talk. What do you say to yourself? Are they words such as" I am sure stupid. That was dumb thing to do. I'm not good enough or smart enough to be part of. ..... I don't deserve to have... ..... Go ahead; one time won't make any difference. Who cares what I do? Nobody loves me."

I could fill pages with these kinds of thoughts, but that would serve no purpose. The truth is we have to love and respect the person we are first, before we are willing to accept the same from others.

If you notice this kind of self-talk stop yourself, and state the opposite. "I do deserve this. Of course I am good enough, Yes that wasn't the smartest thing to do or say, I made a mistake, next time I will know better."

Over time, and with practice, we become less harsh, less judgmental, more tolerant and more forgiving of ourselves. We no longer hold ourselves to impossible, unattainable standards.

Often I tell myself "*I am going to look after me because there are more than enough people out there willing to put me down. I am the only person who knows what's best for me.*"

TIP #3

THE COMFORT ZONE

I used to have a Comfort Zone
Where I knew I wouldn't fail.
The same four walls of busy work,
Were really more like jail.

I longed so much to
Do the things,
I'd never done before.
But I stayed inside my comfort Zone,
And paced the same old floor.

I said it didn't matter,
That I wasn't doing much.
I said I didn't care for things
Like diamonds, furs and such.

I claimed to be so busy
With the things inside my zone,
But deep inside I longed for
Something special of my own.

I couldn't let my life go by
just watching others win.
I held my breath and stepped outside
To let the change begin.

I took a step and with new strength
I'd never felt before.
I kissed my Comfort Zone "goodbye"
And closed and locked the door,

If you are in a Comfort Zone,
Afraid to venture out,
Remember that all winners were
At one time filled with doubt.

A step or two and words of praise
Can make your dreams come true.
Greet your future with a smile,
Success is there for you!

Author Unknown

TIP #4

LIVE BY YOUR VALUES

Each of us has an inner set of rules we use to guide our actions. These rules determine our moral conduct, how we treat other people and animals, and what we believe in. Nearly everything we do is governed by the rules of our personal Value System

Before we can begin to figure out who we are, we have to know what we believe in. Every day we are bombarded with messages that bring into question what is right and wrong, or give us a reason to compromise our beliefs. It is up to us to determine what we believe or what we are willing to take a stand for?

By values I am referring to our beliefs such as:

Loyalty	Honesty	Fairness
Family	Compassion	Sincerity
Integrity	Faith	Independence
Respect	Truthfulness	Dignity

How do we go about figuring out the rules we use to govern our lives? First we need to answer some questions. "Who is the person I respect the most? Why? What qualities do I see in my best friend? What are three things I hate? What three people do I dislike the most and why? What do I do that people compliment me for? What are the three most important qualities I want to pass on to my children or grandchildren? If I were the guest speaker at a high school graduation what would I say to them? What one thing in today's society angers me and why?"

The answers to these questions give us an overview of what we feel is important to us. Some of these values have been instilled in us by others; some we made a conscious decision to follow. The secret is being flexible when we apply them to ourselves. If we are too rigid in our thinking we judge others by what we think or how we feel, not acknowledging that they have their own value system they live by. Often we fail to take into account that others have their own set of values that differ from ours.

I am a sucker for a sob story. One afternoon last summer my phone rang, and a lady introduced herself as a retired nun making a pilgrimage from Toronto to Yellowknife. She had been walking for weeks and needed to rest before she headed north. She asked if I would pay for one night's accommodation at a local motel. Another person had agreed to pay for her first night, but she wanted to stay for a second.

I couldn't say no. Sure, I knew that I was probably being taken in by a con artist, but what if I was in the same situation one day? The other thing I thought of was what if this was Jesus testing me. I gladly paid for her room. My husband Bob simply shook his head. She left the next day and was seen walking north on the highway, pulling her suitcase behind her.

I learned another important lesson that day; people are not always what they appear to be. When I went to the motel to pay for the room the person at the front desk made several disparaging remarks about what had taken place. She digressed about people always taking advantage of them, trying to get cheap rooms or not having to pay at all. She ridiculed me for being stupid enough to fall for this scam.

I thought to myself, *"I see this person at our worship service where we are taught compassion and love for one another. How can she be there yet speak so totally opposite in her daily life."*

Some of you will see me as a hypocrite. How could I see this person at church and write what I just did? That makes me no different than her. As I thought more about this, I realized she had offended my value system, and I failed to recognize that she lived by her own. Neither one of us gave the other credit for doing what we thought was right in this circumstance. The hundred dollars I paid for the room wasn't going to make or break me. I believe in helping others less fortunate than myself. Obviously this woman needed my assistance or she wouldn't have asked. Even if she was scamming me, she must have had a reason for doing so.

When I was a teenager, my parents took in stray teens. These were not foster children, but kids that needed a place to stay for a period of time. They received no pay for this. The kids came and lived with us until their situation improved. They were treated the same as we were, and expected to follow the same rules. Many of those children kept in touch with my parents for years. Now, I think that my dad had been one of these kids, and by taking in these children, he was actually paying forward what had been done for him.

Most of our inner conflicts arise because we are faced with a situation that challenges our values. Basically, we are thinking of doing the opposite of what we believe in.

Two years ago we went to the Bahamas with my daughter, her husband and our three grandchildren. Several times we ate at the same restaurant because the food was good, and the price was right.

One evening, while waiting for our meal to appear, I watched one of the servers open the till, take out several large bills and then put them into her open purse. A person passing by would have thought she had been reaching in for the stick of gum she held in her hand. It was plain to see this wasn't the first time she had done this.

Now I had a dilemma, *"what should I do? Do I mind my own business and pretend I didn't see anything, or do I ask to speak to the manager?"* After a great deal of consideration I said, and did nothing, but you can see my inaction and my conscience still bothers me today? I justified my action because we were eating in a casino restaurant, and there must have been are all kinds of cameras scattered around. What should I have done? What would have been the right thing to do? I still don't know. How would you have handled this situation if you were in my place?

I guess what I am trying to pass along is that we need to follow what we believe in and do what we think is right for us. We already know the difference between right and wrong. The harder path to travel is the one that we know is right, but in doing so, puts us at odds with others around us. It is choosing to do what is right over what is easy or convenient. In the end, we are the ones who have to live with our conscience.

TIP #5

HONOUR YOURSELF

One of the most useful books ever written, beside the Bible, is the dictionary. When I'm not sure of a word I get out my trusty old Funk and Wagnall and look up the meaning. Usually what I think a word means, and what it actually means, are two different things.

When my coach first mentioned the phrase "Honor Yourself" I didn't have a clue what she was talking about. I found the word honor means having a clear sense of right or wrong: showing great respect to, or holding in high regard. After thinking about this for some time, I realized that I didn't hold myself in high regard, nor did I respect the woman I am.

Throughout my childhood I was told "children should be seen but not heard." The safest way was to keep my mouth shut, and not draw attention to what I was doing. Be a team player, not a leader. I found I could work effectively in the background without calling attention to myself. This worked for a long time but, and there is always a but, the time came when I wanted to speak out, and make my voice heard.

In order to honor who I was, I had to start looking after me. I had to be conscious of my own spiritual, emotional, mental and physical needs. I had to begin asking myself the tough questions. *"Is this good for me? Is this person good to have in my life right now? What do I need right now, today? What is my first step?"*

Honoring ourselves is giving ourselves what we freely give to others. If we give out love, respect, understanding, patience, belief, praise and recognition to those around us, why are we so reluctant to do the same for ourselves? Why do we hold ourselves to a standard that is nearly impossible to live up to?

I don't know about you, but I am a recovering perfectionist. If I am asked to do something, I usually try to go above and beyond what is expected. I've never been a believer in doing something half way. Even a simple errand, such as going to the grocery store for my mother-in-law involved finding exactly what was on the list at the best price. If she wanted two bananas, I found the best two.

Trying to be a perfectionist has led to nothing but frustration. One of my challenges became trying not to do everything perfect and still honor what I was doing. When I am tired or overwhelmed, I easily fall back into this old habit because then I feel that I am in control.

At the end of my Direct Sales career I was frustrated and very unhappy. I had attained a new position in management; one I aspired to and dreamed about for years, but it was a hollow victory. The time had come to face reality and honestly answer the one question haunting me *"was I ready to put in the time and effort necessary to rebuild my Unit?"*

My new offspring Director took with her the women she had shared her business with. That was the way the business was set up, and I didn't have a problem with that, but essentially I was starting over. Did I really want to work that hard again?

The truth was NO, I didn't want to. New horizons were opening up for me. My sales career no longer fulfilled the reasons I had for beginning in the first place.

My aspirations were leading me in a different direction.

I chose to retire. I honored what was best for me by asking the questions, and being completely honest with my answer. The time had come to move on. After twenty one years I wanted to pursue something different in my life. By admitting the truth to myself, I became free to do something I loved, something that stirred my deepest passion and fulfilled my purpose.

Over time, I realized I was a grown woman, had raised four children, held responsible positions in the community, and I was perfectly capable of making my own decisions. Yet it was tough. Learning to care about me, and giving myself permission to do so was harder than I thought it would be. I was used to discounting my thoughts and keeping my opinions to myself, but I am learning. I still get a great deal of satisfaction from putting my time and effort into others, but now I understand the motivation behind my actions.

As we learn to love and appreciate who we really are, we learn to give ourselves what we need. As we accept ourselves, warts and all, we become the person God plans us to be.

I am not who I was,
Nor have I become all I am destined to be.
My journey lies in accepting the challenges of today.

TIP #6

CHANGE IS INEVITABLE. ACCEPT IT

For the sake of clarity, so that we both understand the meanings of certain terms I am using I once again opened my trusty old dictionary:

Ending – the last part, death, conclusion: the point where something ceases to be.

Beginning – come into being: the first part of doing something; to get something going.

Faith – believing without proof

Hope – the expectation that something desired will happen

Trust - a firm belief in the honesty, truthfulness, justice or power of a person or thing.

Metamorphosis – change of character, appearance or condition.

Change – become different; lack of sameness; put one thing in place of another.

Each day of our lives we have the opportunity to start over, utilizing the processes of change and choice. Think of a butterfly. This beautiful insect begins its life as a lowly caterpillar eating leaves, crawling around in the grass and maturing. Then one day, by instinct, it encases itself in a fuzzy cocoon and waits. Finally the day arrives when, through struggle and challenge, it casts off its cocoon and emerges as a butterfly An insect crawled upon a branch, and after a life or death struggle, emerged to fly free of the bonds that held it. In the process, its physical appearance changed, but it is the same unique creature God made. Also, the butterfly would wither and die if we helped it emerge from its cocoon. It's the struggle that makes it strong enough to survive.

I am one of those people who find adjusting to change a major challenge. I am safe, comfortable, and my life is predictable. I want everything to remain exactly the way it is, but change is inevitable because people and circumstances are forever evolving. The world is changing, and in most cases, I need to change too or be left behind.

Take something as simple as a telephone. Many years ago my number was 42. To call long distance I dialed 0 to get an operator. Next, I received a seven digit number, then a ten digit number. Not only could I dial long distance myself, I could dial any place in the world. From rotary dial to push button to Skype, from land line to mobile to cell phone to Android. Along the way I had to embrace the changes. That doesn't mean I liked them, but I had no choice, I had to move along with the times and evolution.

My old rotary phone will still work to a degree, but to communicate I need to use what is current – I-phones, I-pads, 4G networks, where will this go next? Who knows, I am still trying to figure out how to set the time on my VCR.

Change occurs in our lives on a daily basis. Some are subtle, others are not. Some of the things we used to be able to do in a short period of time now take twice as long and are twice as complicated. Last week I went to the bank to deposit some money into my grandson's bank account for him to use while in school. The teller refused to take my money unless I had his account number. I thought providing his name and other pertinent information would be far more reliable and safer than just his account number.

I looked at her incredulously and said, "Are you serious?" She was very serious, but finally allowed me to make the deposit. Go figure!

Some of the more profound changes we experience such as the death of child or spouse, losing a breast to cancer, a job loss, a sudden move, the breakup of a marriage, hearing a loved one has a potentially fatal disease are thrust upon us, and we are forced to make changes whether we want to or not. Now we need to try to understand, accept and adapt. We know life will be different than it was, but we are uncertain what the future holds. We can't go back, but are reluctant or afraid to move forward. This is the reason I started this chapter with the definitions that I did. I wish I had understood the process earlier, because I could have saved myself a lot of grief.

An ending is something that ceases to be in the same form. That part is over, done, kaput, and no more. When one thing ends, something new comes and fills the void and we, are left with the hope that whatever is coming will be better. We try to believe this is happening for our own good, and trust in our Higher Power to show us the way. We need assurance that all of our tears and suffering are leading us to a better good. Like the butterfly, our metamorphosis begins, and before we know it we are living with the changes.

A very close friend was diagnosed with breast cancer

during her routine yearly mammogram. She was immediately plunged into the world of specialists, biopsy, surgery, and chemotherapy. In one thousandth of a second, the time it took to photograph the imprint of her breast on an x-ray film, her world changed.

Her attitude quickly went from placidly going through life to fighting for her life. Although I am sure she mourned the loss of her breast and femininity, her very existence was under siege. She did what was necessary, and did so with a very positive spirit. I will always admire her for how she handled this difficult situation.

One day she phoned and asked if I would like to go boob shopping with her in Grande Prairie. Her first purchase was prosthesis and several new bras, and then we went sweater shopping. That day, through those simple acts, she went from being a victim of breast cancer to a survivor.

I saw her a few days later wearing one of her new sweaters. I went up to her and said "looking good girl."

She grinned, stuck out her chest and replied, "Feels good too."

We need to have enough faith to believe our current struggle will end, that it has been worthwhile, and that our future will benefit from our experience. I remember being told once upon a time "keep telling yourself that this too shall pass." Things change, nothing lasts forever.

My friend's old way of living had ended, now she is in a different place, and what happened in between was the learning, the growing and adapting to the changes.

Try to remind yourself that while you are learning, you can't make a mistake. If one avenue doesn't work, you are free to seek another, and then another until you get what you are looking for. If you mess up, you have discovered one more way that doesn't produce the results you are looking for, and this becomes part of your learning curve.

Some lessons take longer than others to learn. Some keep repeating themselves over and over until we finally get the message. Life continues to be a circle of endings, learning and beginnings. Changes will continually challenge us throughout our journey, and we will spend much of our time trying to adapt to them.

I don't know if you can easily accept the fact that all of our hurts and struggles are worthwhile. During this process, we are becoming who we are meant to be. Sometimes life just plain sucks and we don't want to go through the learning process. But, like the butterfly, we need these challenges to make us stronger. Years may pass before we fully appreciate the value of our experience. Sometimes change is devastating. There are no answers, and possibly never will be. All we can do is move on the best we can.

The more we resent the letting go of our old ways, the more difficult we make life for ourselves. As cynical as this may sound, very few people care about the drama taking place in our lives. They have their own "stuff" to go through. We walk on parallel paths, in some cases we could be going through the same experience, but our learning is focused on what is necessary for us.

Change can be as difficult as we make it. Even though I have found myself wanting change, even willing change, I resisted. In the end, I did finally learn to accept that what was before is now gone. For the change to be successful, for things to really be different, I had to learn to live with the new. One thing for sure, I couldn't spend my time going around second guessing every decision I made. I simply made the best of the situation. I mean what else could I do?

We often feel hurt, disillusioned and angry. We don't want to go through the process, but we have no choice. I have learned to think only to the next step. First we do this, next we do that, and so on. This way I can accept each change that comes on an individual basis. I am empowering myself to remain calm, to think, and not allow my fear to overpower me like a runaway train.

The simplicity of living with change is considering what is best for us from the beginning. Making an effort one day at a time, one attempt at a time, or one step at a time will alter our life experiences. This is a process, and we need to learn to appreciate each step we take

Compare change to building a house of bricks. Every day you add one more brick. Soon you have one wall, then two, then four and eventually a house. Some weeks you add a few, others you add many. As long as you keep on adding bricks you will get the desired result.

Change thrust upon us is different because we are forced to accept what is. We can go with the flow of the river or battle the stream; we always have the freedom to choose which path to follow. The one constancy in our life is change. Fortunately, God has given us the ability to choose how we will react and determine what effect the change is going to have upon us. In the end we are like the butterfly, we are reborn into something better and more beautiful.

TIP #7

TAKE CHARGE OF CHANGE

We are creatures of habit, going through our daily routine, doing the same things in the same way. If one little thing changes we get upset.

Every weekend, during the summer, friends of ours go camping, and for more than fifteen years they have camped in the exact same spot. They have a predictable routine; the only variation is the cast of characters who stop by to visit. Most of the locals leave the spot open for them, but a stranger wouldn't know. I have often wondered what would happen if they arrived one Friday night to find somebody else in their spot. I don't know if they would go so far as to ask them to move, but I do know that couple would be upset all weekend.

For some of us change is very difficult, our security disappears and we are left fearing the perils of the unknown. Several years ago we decided we were going to spend part of the winter in Arizona with another couple, and then a series of mishaps occurred that upset our plans. The fellow we were planning on going with unexpectedly died, our daughter and son-in-law separated and my little dog got run over. Each of these events produced a change in my orderly little world.

My husband Bob and I decided to go for a month anyway, but instead of taking our trailer, we would drive. As the time approached, I began to have misgivings, but didn't say anything because I didn't want to hurt his feelings. I knew he was looking forward to the trip. Instead of speaking up, I kept telling myself I was being silly and that everything would be OK. By the time we were a hundred miles from home I was in the throes of a full blown panic attack.

If you have ever had this experience you can relate to how I was feeling. Every nerve in my body was vibrating from fear, my heart was pounding, and I couldn't get my breath. We turned around and came home.

Still today as I look back, I don't understand why I had such an extreme reaction. I was sick the day we left, so the question becomes was it an allergic reaction to the medication or old fashioned fear? Were there too many changes at one time, or was I afraid of speaking up and saying "I would rather stay home." My biggest regret is not speaking up and not being open and honest about how I felt. My home is my security blanket, and with all of the changes that occurred I wasn't feeling safe. Oh; the things we do to ourselves.

In this case, fear represented the unknown. The "what ifs" entered my thinking. "What if we had an accident? What if we ended up losing everything we have worked so hard for because I was sick? What if I spoke up and he stopped loving me?"

We easily understand the logistics of change, but we also need to address the human and emotional responses. Lately I have done some reading about the effects of change. One article I read said that people respond to change in a fearful way by exhibiting behaviors such as withdrawal, aggressiveness, avoidance, micro-managing, paralysis or denial.

In another article I read, "If you keep doing things the same way you have always done them, you will keep getting the same result." I believe this is one of the definitions of insanity.

When we enter into something new, it is perfectly normal to have doubts. Have I made the right decision? Could I have done this differently? If not attended to, these doubts can begin a downward spiral that ends up paralyzing us. We become unable to act or make a decision, fear sets in. Does any of this sound familiar?

An article in the Edmonton Journal from the year 2000 suggested ways to deal with our emotional responses to change. I will paraphrase them for you:

1. Have a systematic way to deal with your doubt. Ask yourself questions like am I certain this is what I should do?
2. If you are uncertain, ask yourself the following questions. What am I hesitant about? Why don't I feel confident? Have I missed something? Is there a different way? When I feel like this I get out my journal, write down the questions, and then write what I am thinking as my answer. Eventually everything becomes clearer, and I can say I am hesitant because...............
3. Now that you know why you are hesitant, on a separate page begin writing solutions. When Dr. Robert Schueller was building the Crystal Cathedral in California he needed one hundred thousand dollars. He took a piece of paper and listed ways he could get this money: one person could give a hundred thousand dollars, two people could each give fifty thousand and so on. In the end he chose to find one hundred people willing to donate one thousand dollars each, and then began his

fund raising campaign on this basis.

4. Doubt can be managed, but if you wait until the stars align themselves perfectly, you will never get started. How much risk are you willing to take? You set the parameters, choosing those that will allow you to start without fear and provide a point where you can stop if you need or want to.

5. Make corrections along the way. Follow the ideas that have worked, and minimize the impact of those that haven't. More than once I have gotten this far then defeated myself by trying to force what I wanted to happen. I also got stuck in "paralysis by analysis," and would spend hours attempting to determine my best course of action. Eventually, I would give up and start over when all I needed to do was take one idea and act upon it. If that idea didn't work, I could have tried another and so on until I found the one that did.

6. Get help if you can't figure out a solution yourself, or if your doubts freeze you. Talk with a friend. Get an idea from someone who has been in a similar situation. Brainstorm ideas on paper.

7. The last step is the most crucial. Do Something. Get to work. Take action. Pick the simplest task and do it for ten minutes. Often you will find that you become energized, your doubts disappear, and when the time is up, you keep on going.

Change creates doubt. With these few simple steps we become surer about what we are doing. Doubt turning to anxiety creates fear. My doubt about leaving home for a month was simply fear of the unknown. Until we face reality and recognize what we are really afraid of, our situation will continue to worsen. Like a virus, our fear will eventually spread to every aspect of our life.

When a person takes action, the universe has something to respond to, and that response lets you know if you are on the right track. A positive response encourages us to keep on going. A negative response means we have to try a different tactic.

Every change gives us an opportunity to learn something new.. Rather than fear these changes, what if we embraced them, and anticipated the new dimensions they would bring to our lives?

TIP #8

MAKE A GOOD FIRST IMPRESSION

Once a year my Direct Selling team and I would set up a booth at a local trade fair to showcase our products and meet new people. During this time we looked and acted as the professionals Beauty Consultants we were trained to be.

I found this to be an excellent time to "people watch." Some were heavier, skinnier, taller, shorter, some prettier, others plainer, blonder, darker, but I noticed a common theme. The clothes they wore seemed to reflect their level of confidence. Some women shuffled past in their sweat pants or pajama bottoms, their head down looking at the floor, and never making any eye contact. They carried an aura of sadness and defeat around them. Others projected sadness as though they carried the weight of the world on their shoulders. Their smiles never reached their eyes.

Some, though wearing the standard jeans and t-shirt, carried an air of exuberance, fun, and appeared to be full of self-confidence. Clearly they loved life. Just being in their presence made you feel better. They carried themselves tall and looked happy.

Some of the exhibitors didn't look professional, nor did they appear enthusiastic about their company or product. They sat staring straight ahead, discouraging a passerby from stopping. If they were going to successfully promote their booth or services first impressions were critical. I always wondered why they paid the big dollars for the booth then wasted the opportunity.

My heart went out to those who appeared so sad, and so defeated. It was like they had given up, and were merely putting in time and waiting - for what I don't know.

We owe it to ourselves to put our best forward every day, in every way we can. Physically this means wearing an attractive hairstyle, a touch of color in our makeup, and clothes that fit properly, and are right for the occasion. They don't need to be expensive but neat, clean and repaired as necessary.

Have you ever watched the television show "What Not to Wear?" Women are transformed in front of our eyes. They are given a five thousand dollar credit card to purchase clothes that enhance their body features. The principle transformation occurs when they began to see themselves in a totally different way. They began to see their bodies, not as something to be ashamed of, but as a confident extension of who they are. Add haircuts that brought out their best features, a few basic make up tips and their confidence suddenly began to bloom. Many struggled during this transformation because they are forced to come out of hiding and face their insecurities.

Many of us feel exactly the same way about ourselves. We hide our bodies in clothing that is too big or unflattering, hoping that nobody will pay attention to us. Have you ever noticed that when you look your worst, you run into someone you have wanted to meet or impress? Happens to me all the time!

If I am going to be working in public I get up, get dressed, and get cute before I leave the house. I take special care choosing what to wear and how I look. If I am staying home I'm not as careful about what I put on, and often end up in my oldest pants and old ratty sweat shirt. I tell myself who cares? Nobody is going to see me anyway. These are the days I feel dispirited and can't figure out why. We all sense, at one time or another, that when we look good, we feel good about ourselves.

First impressions also come from our demeanor, as well as how we look. Another impression killer is the words that come out of our mouths. Many people sprinkle their conversations with profanity, and some words personally offend me. I admit I have been known to use the odd swear words, but some go too far. The other day I heard a comment about a young woman that nearly broke my heart. "She is such a beautiful young lady. It's hard to believe the filth spewing from her mouth." This young lady has been judged on how she sounds, not on the fact she is intelligent and attractive.

Bob and I were talking about this the other day. He said "if a man uses profanity, people tend to overlook it. When a woman uses the same words it is demeaning, unflattering and invalidating "

Once again the double standard appears, but I see his point. Somehow it seems sad that many girls and woman resort to foul language as a means of gaining attention. To me, this foul language is one more piece of evidence that the woman has little respect for herself.

The best way to make a first impression is to smile. They are free, and need no special wrapping to give them away. As a child, I was told a smile is a frown turned upside down. When we smile at someone we usually get one back. We find it hard to stay gloomy when we are smiling.

People want to be seen, and to be acknowledged. They don't want to be just another face in the crowd. Greeting them with a smile makes them feel noticed. They carry their head a little higher and begin passing these smiles along. A smile from a stranger always brightens our day.

Mary Kay Ash often said "each person wears a sign saying make me feel special." One of the simplest ways to do this is to call someone by their first name. This is much easier in a retail setting if the person in front of you is wearing a name tag, but if you don't know their name, take a second, look them in the eye and say thank you. You will make them feel appreciated.

One day I was in Walmart waiting to pay for my purchases and the customer in front of me was arguing with the cashier over the prices of several articles. She thought the price should be lower than what the cashier had rang up in her till. The cashier doesn't know the price of every article that passes in front of her, and has to rely on what has been downloaded into her computer.

Eventually, a supervisor came over, went to the bin, checked the actual price of the articles, came back, and tried to explain to the customer that the tag was correct. Somehow the contents of two bins had become mixed up.

The customer picked up the articles, threw them at the cashier, swore at her and walked out of the store. That poor girl was close to tears by the time she finished voiding the whole order. My heart went out to her. When she had finished running my few things through the till, I said "I saw how the customer before me gave you a bad time. I congratulate you on the way you handled the situation. You did a good job."

"This is my first day," she said, brightening up and smiling back.

It always feels good when we give or receive a sincere compliment, a smile, or a thank you. The world doesn't center on us alone; although there are times we want to think it does. Acknowledging others benefits two people, the giver and the receiver. Two spirits are uplifted during this brief exchange.

TIP #9

MAKE ME FEEL SPECIAL

Many years ago we went through a traumatic event which deeply impacted our family and business. Our oldest son had an accident that left him burned, and destroyed our main fuel truck.

He was flown to the Burn Unit in Edmonton where he stayed for a month with fifteen to twenty percent of his body covered in second and third degree burns. The truck had exploded and was unrecognizable, but miraculously he had crawled out to the road before this happened.

Sometimes situations occur in our lives which force us to look at our priorities, In this case buying a new truck, dealing with insurance, finding another driver and travelling three hundred miles back and forth to visit him took precedence over everything else.

I put my direct sales business on hold. It seemed incongruous that selling skin care and make up was as important as our son. He needed reassurance that we weren't angry with him. I used to tell him," Accidents happen. They make fuel trucks every day, but you are the one that is important to us." At that point I was seriously considering closing my business.

During this time, one of the other Consultants in our area phoned and asked for my assistance. She was going to the group home for severely handicapped children and adults, and needed an extra pair of hands. Naturally I said yes. I had no desire to go, but everyone else had turned her down.

The young lady I was to work with was severely

handicapped, confined to a wheel chair, and unable to speak. Her movements were spastic and she cried out at odd times. She was completely incapable of doing anything for herself.

I began by smoothing cleanser on her face followed by the facial mask. Almost immediately I noticed she was becoming calmer, and then I felt her pushing her head against my hand. It took me a few seconds to realize that I was comforting her by stroking her face.

Very slowly I applied the freshener and moisturizer, taking extra time to gently stroke her. She became very still. For a few minutes there was only the two of us in the room, me stroking her cheek, and her head leaning into my hand with her eyes closed. This magical moment was all too soon broken by the confusion around us. At the time, I wondered how long it had been since someone had taken the time to touch her, other than for feeding or cleaning. Her physical body had betrayed her, but her soul still needed the caring touch of another person.

Some of you may think that it was a good of me to take the time to spend with her, but if the truth be known, that young lady gave me the greatest gift she had to offer. She made me feel special. She showed me that she appreciated the touch of my hand the only way she knew how.

I don't know if she ever knew the powerful effect she had on me, or how she helped change my thinking. Yes, we were going through a rough time. Yes, our son was burned, but we still had him. He would recover to live a fruitful life. This child would never have that opportunity.

I realized living isn't always about money or being part

of the rat race we are caught up in. Living is touching the lives of others, freely offering them whatever we have to give. Living is about making our world a better place.

Shortly after that I returned to my business, but my perception was different. Selling the products and recovering my investment was still important, but no longer my priority. I wanted, for the short period of time I was with my client, to make her feel better about herself. If I could do that, then I had accomplished what I set out to do.

This young lady has since passed to a better place, but if I could, I would say to her, "thank you for making me feel special, you changed my life." I hope now that she is an angel who can walk and play, speak and be happy. Her frail body gave me a gift that can never be measured.

TIP#10

FIND BALANCE

Sometimes I think I exhibit the symptoms of OCD (obsessive Compulsive disorder). When I begin a project I spend long periods of time entirely focused on what I am doing to the exclusion of everything else.

For twenty years Sales was my life. Everything I did revolved around what was necessary to make my business successful. I was a tough task master to work for, hard on myself with higher than normal expectations.

There were times I longed for a feeling of peace in my life - time to relax, and let go of all the responsibilities. As I write this I have finally come aware that the peace I was seeking is called balance.

The words to an old song sang by Rosemary Clooney enter my head "work eight hours, sleep eight hours, have eight hours of fun." How is that for dating myself? Any way I couldn't turn off my head, I was always working and forgot to have fun in my life.

For the sixteen years we ran our fuel distribution business we both felt like we were working 24/7. Once a year, on the July long weekend, we took an extra day off to visit some good friends. We justified taking this time because the crops were seeded, and the haying hadn't quite started. Just like the farmers, we were governed by the season of the year. We also took a couple of days in February to go to our Agents meeting, but that was more work than pleasure.

We all need down time to relax, to connect with others, to reconnect with our soul. Today most of us would have to schedule this in. We are afraid to turn off our cell phones or tablets because we might miss something. We are afraid to be disconnected from our world. We forget that our lives are happening in the NOW, because we are too busy doing something else, such as texting or following Facebook.

You may be thinking "I know what you are saying, but I don't have time." In some ways I agree with you, but sometimes we are so busy doing, that we fail to take time to value and appreciate what we already have.

Perhaps there was a time your child came to you and said, "mommy please read me a story," but you were busy making supper. This is one of the most challenging times of a day, and the last thing you have time for is reading a story. You put her off by saying "after supper," but something else comes up and the story is forgotten. In actuality the five minutes spent reading the story would have been more valuable than making sure supper was on time.

I can't tell you how many times I wish I could go back to when my kids were little. I would have spent less time worrying about money and bills, and spent more time living in the NOW with them. I was one of the lucky ones. When my children were small, I worked part time and was home with them, yet I feel I missed something.

We used to have a very large white and yellow striped semi-circular chair. All of the kids plus me could fit into it. Most evenings, before bed, we sat in this chair and watched TV or I would read to them. Now I look back and fully appreciate those moments.

Each of us is given the same twenty four hours a day.

What is important is how we fill them. Do we choose to fill them with the mundane or with quality? Mary Kay Ash always suggested that our priorities should be "God first, family second, career last". Of course there are short periods of time when one or the other takes precedence, but when these periods are over, it's important to regain the balance in our daily life. For many of us our work consumes our time, but in actuality none of us are indispensable. We want to think we are, but the truth is the work will continue to get done whether we are there or not.

Take time to breathe deeply and find balance in your life. Carve out time for fun and relaxation in your frantic schedule. Turn off your cell phone. Take time to laugh, play and feel joy for a few minutes every day. Our best memories come from the fun times we share, so my best advice is to make a memory today.

TIP #11

BE GENTLE WITH YOURSELF

Often we are our own worst enemy instead of being our best friend. I feel this is especially true when we have been traumatized, when we are left questioning who and what we believe in. These are the times we have been shaken to our core, and no longer know what is true and what isn't.

I hope my husband will forgive me when he reads this but here goes anyway. He was the foreman of a crew of men who maintained the secondary highways in our area. Usually the crew consisted of twelve trucks, the drivers and other workers. He had been doing this job for five years and was proud of his men and their accomplishments. Every summer they worked hard, spending long weeks away from their home and families.

Toward the end of the fifth year, a new Supervisor was hired for his department. He was twenty years younger with a "know it all" attitude. He had never done this type of work before, whereas Bob had spent more than thirty years involved with road construction of some sort.

The clash was inevitable. By the middle of June, the following year my husband quit his job. Day after day he was cursed and screamed at. He couldn't get his trucks fixed when they broke down, then he was reprimanded for not getting the work done fast enough. Anyone who knows Bob will tell you that he is usually a laid back person, never gets overly excited, and handles pressure well.

The man I was now living with wasn't the same one I had spent the last forty years with. Personally, I was happy when he quit because that was a better alternative than a heart attack. He was hurt, his self-esteem damaged, and he was very angry. I am well aware this sounds like sour grapes, but we went through a difficult time for a few months.

The one thing he needed was validation, that he had done a good job for the company. He needed to know that he was still capable of being productive, and that his supervisor should have treated him with respect. I couldn't give this to him, but I wished I could.

The first time I heard the term validation I wasn't sure of what the meaning was so I looked it up. To paraphrase my trusty old dictionary, to validate something is to prove true and correct, to confirm as the truth or rightness. Going through this difficult time rocked his feelings of self-worth. He needed confirmation for himself that all the time and effort he had put into his work was important and of value.

I began to see that the need for validation can take many forms. The person who hops from bed to bed seeking love, or finding acceptance in a bottle or a needle are seeking a way to find value in their life. One of our basic human needs is love, and when this is withdrawn, we will do whatever we feel is necessary to seek and find what we are looking for.

I clearly see now that the rejection from my siblings was behind my efforts to do and be there for everyone. Not understanding this concept I put myself through hell. I thought the opinion of my family was true; I never once thought they were mistaken. If they didn't want me then who would? I needed something that made me feel I was important and worthy so I went out of my way.

I think most of us face something similar to this situation at one time or another during our life. We feel broken, disconnected, and that the people we have trusted and put our faith in have let us down. Our comfort zone is shattered. We begin beating ourselves up, taking blame for circumstances that were beyond our control.

This is the when we need to stop and be gentle with ourselves. We need to become our own best friend. We need to provide our spirits with a sanctuary, something that allows us the time and space to heal. Somehow we need to find a way to give ourselves the validation we are looking for.

There are many ways we can do this, read the bible, seek solace in our faith, meditation, take long walks communing with nature, or join a support group and so on. Most of all, we have to stop blaming ourselves and accept the facts as they are. "It is what it is," and there is little we can do to make it different. Any form of destructive behavior compounds our problem, isolating us even more. If the truth be known, we aren't nearly as bad, or dumb or lazy or hurt as we think we are.

Traumatic events often affect us for years because of the changes they bring. We learn to cope with the physical changes, but we also must learn that we don't have to allow what happened in the past define who we are for the rest of our lives.

When you are going through a difficult time, remember that there are people who love you for who you are, just the way you are. Draw comfort from them.

TIP #12

FIND YOUR QUIET PLACE

Our lives today can get pretty crazy. In this era of instant communication we have little time to be quiet, to think. We expect ourselves to be this super person who can do or be everything to everyone all of the time. When we go on a vacation, we usually come home more tired than when we left. Inevitably we run out of steam.

Is there a special time or place you can recall that brings you a feeling of peace or happiness? I would like you to search your memory bank for such a place. Did you find it? I have two such places I visit to regain that tranquil feeling; one is the ocean, the other sitting in front of a campfire.

I love the ocean, the sound of the waves lapping onto the shore, watching the ebb and flow of the tide, the feeling of the sand being dragged out from under my feet. The first time I had this experience was on a quiet beach in Hawaii. As I stood in the water, I could feel the strong current and see how high the waves were. The water, as it rushed back to the sea, was pulling the sand from under my feet and I felt like I was being propelled forward. The water splashed high on my thighs; the Hawaiian sun warmed my skin. I thought that if there is a heaven, this must be it.

Many years later I was standing on a beach in the Bahamas. The waves were gentler, the current weaker, but once again I got that same feeling. This is what life is all about.

I could hear my grandchildren laughing as the waves washed away their sand castles. I walked out knee high into the water, and stood with my arms stretched sideways, my eyes closed, taking in the warmth of the sun, the sounds of the waves and the feeling of complete peace. I wanted to be able to remember this moment for the rest of my life.

My second place of retreat came one evening as I gazed into our campfire. That night the conditions were perfect. It was dark, the Milky Way seemed so close and bright that I felt that I could reach up and count each individual star. A soft gentle breeze was blowing. I don't know what kind of wood was burning, but there were a lot of sparks. I was mesmerized as I watched the tiny red embers escape the fire, twisting, and turning, floating higher and higher into the night sky until they disappeared. I could hear the crackle of the flames, and my friends laughing in the background as I watched natures fireworks display. Even as I am writing about this I feel that same peaceful feeling wash over me.

Jennie taught me a simple way to return to these places when I need a brief respite from life, and this what I wish to share with you today. First, turn off the TV, radio, your cell phone, anything that may distract you. Find a quiet comfortable place to sit or lie. Once you are settled, picture yourself standing on the top step of a beautiful stair case. At the top is the craziness of your world, at the bottom is that quiet place I asked you to find. Visualize beautiful flowers planted along the sides of each step. Smell the fragrant perfume. Take several deep breaths and exhale slowly. Now begin to descend the steps one step at a time, pausing to rest and breathe on each one. Continue to breathe slowly and evenly.

As you slowly walk down the steps allow the stress and tension to drain away. Continue until you reach your quiet spot at the bottom of the stairs. Stand there, reliving your previous experience. Enjoy those feelings of peace and contentment, assure yourself that your world is perfect just the way it is. When you are ready, begin walking slowly back up the stairs carrying this peaceful relaxed feeling with you. When you reach the top, take one more deep breathe, then open your eyes. How do you feel?

In the short time you were gone not much changed in your stressful demanding world, but you are changed. Your inner self feels more peaceful, and you feel better equipped to handle the craziness surrounding you.

I have also used this technique when faced with a difficult decision. At the top I express my problem to the universe, and then slowly go down the stairs allowing my subconscious mind to work its magic. Often by the time I reach the bottom, I have a solution to my problem. As I walk back up the stairs my unconscious mind mulls this over, and by the time I have reached the top, I have usually decided what my next step should be.

I have used this when I am having one of those nights and can't fall asleep. As I walk down the stairs I will my body to relax and my mind to slow down. Often I am asleep before I reach the bottom step.

I really don't know if this will work for you, but it's worth a try. The first few times it's hard to maintain the concentration because the things we need to do keep crowding into our mind. We find it hard to let go. We tell ourselves we don't have time for this, but practice makes perfect. The more times we attempt to reach the peacefulness of our quiet spot, the easier it becomes.

Your special places or feelings may be very different than mine. Maybe yours is a time you felt like one with the wind as it blew through your hair. Maybe it was the time you held your sleeping child in your arms, or you sat by a waterfall and let the thundering noise and rushing water carry your problems away. Wherever your place is, I urge you to visit it as often as you can.

TIP #13

MAKE A CHOICE

Now I find it hard to believe, but at one time I didn't realize I had a choice about a lot of things in my life. I was brought up in the environment, "Do what you are told and don't you dare question my authority."

The rebel inside would taunt me saying, "You don't have to listen to them. You can do whatever you want," but I usually conceded to the, "as long as you live in my house you will do what I say," rule to keep the peace

I don't know if you can imagine the freedom I felt when I found out I could choose whether to do this or that. I could say yes or no, I could go if I wanted, or I could choose to stay home. I could wear bright red lipstick or soft pink. If I wanted to, I could paint my toes with bright purple nail polish. I no longer needed to justify to myself every choice I made.

I was fifteen when my dad picked me up from school, drove me home, and then beat me because he was angry about something I had done. The bruises on my body eventually faded, but the bruise on my soul is only now beginning to heal. After that incident I made sure I followed the rules – well most of the time anyway. Besides, I figured what he didn't know wouldn't hurt him, and I also decided it was easier to beg for forgiveness then to ask and be told no.

I wasn't allowed to go to my grade twelve graduation party because there would be drinking, but I went anyway. Yes, there was drinking but I didn't. I was already in enough trouble for going, without having the smell of alcohol on my breath when I got home. My fondest memory of that night is of all the boys peeing on the fire to make sure the flames were out. I think I was grounded for the rest of my life, but it was worth it.

The night before I moved north to work, my friends held a going away party for me. That was the one and only time I ever drank lemon gin, and then I refused to go home until I was completely sober. My curfew was midnight, but I never got home until seven in the morning. To this day I can't stand the smell or taste of lemon gin.

My dad was waiting for me at the door in his full Irish fury. I looked at him and said, "If you touch me I won't be back. I leave tonight, and what you do determines if I stay away for good or come home again." Those were pretty brave words coming from someone shaking in her boots with fear. I had broken three rules; don't talk back, no drinking and be home by midnight.

Here I was, a high school graduate being treated like a young teenager. I was nineteen years old and had completed my training as a Laboratory and X-Ray Technician. My instructor had found a placement for me in a hospital where I in charge of two departments yet wasn't allowed to stay out past midnight. There was something very wrong with this picture. I hated sneaking around, but I hated being controlled every moment more. My words must have hit home because he turned and walked away from me. That evening, when he drove me to the bus station there were tears in his eyes. I'm positive that, for the first time, he realized I was all grown up.

Thanks to the Hippie movement and the Women's Lib movement of the early 70's women now have choices not previously available to them. Now we can be an astronaut or a stay at home parent. Gone are the days when the only choices available were to be a nurse, a secretary, a teacher, a sales clerk or stay at home wife and mother. We have the freedom to do and be anything we wish,

The other side of the choice coin is that we are responsible for the results of our choices. Maybe we made a good choice, maybe we didn't, but whatever the result, we have to live with it.

At times my inability to choose, to make any kind of decision, has left me in the position of doing nothing, because I didn't know what to do, or was afraid to take the risk. That was also a choice which meant that nothing changed, and that things would remain the same as they were.

We make simple choices each and every day. Some appear to be nothing; while others are mind blowing or life altering. The thing is we are never sure where our choice will take us.

My biggest revelation of all was that I was free to allow who or what I wanted to happen in my life. Wow! A new amazing world opened up. No more long explanations trying to defend myself, no more doing things because I was told to. Today, this is my definition of freedom.

Miracles begin to appear when we make our personal choices within the context of the question, "is this good for me at this time?" Some choices are no brainers, but other times the choices are hard, and the consequences unclear. We may be the abused wife or child asking ourselves "do I stay or do I go?" Am I still willing to put up with this, or should I walk away? Should I tell someone what is happening to me or should I remain quiet?

My point is, you can make your own choice, because that is what you want, and for no other good reason, knowing that you have to live with the consequences. If we make a wrong choice it doesn't necessarily mean it's the end of the world or will be that way forever. Our future choices can be redirected in such a way as to rectify the situation. We also have the option of changing our mind if we wish to.

Each of us has a choice in any given situation. While writing this, I thought some of you might say "I beg to differ. It wasn't my choice that my husband passed away in a car accident. What choice did I have in that?"

You didn't have a choice in what happened, but you do have a choice in how you respond. You can decide to make the best of your situation or decide not to. You can to choose go on living or stay stuck. It's entirely up to you.

When my brother was dying, his young sons phoned me. "Auntie, we don't know what to do. The radiation isn't helping dad and he is suffering so much. We know that he isn't going to get better."

"What do you feel you should do?" I replied.

"We want to stop the radiation and let him go in peace."

"Do what you think your dad would want you to do. Talk this over with your mom, and whatever you decide, don't let anyone to criticize you for it. Once you have made your decision, don't even question yourself. You do what you think is right," was my reply to them.

This was hard on two young men in their early 20's. In the end, they chose to stop the treatments, keep him comfortable and let him go. As far as I am concerned this was the right choice. He was in excruciating pain until he lapsed into a coma. I am sure my brother smiles down on them, and is very proud of the young men they have become. I am too! I know that in this particular circumstance, their decision was based on the love they felt for their dad, and their wish for him not to suffer any more.

I encourage you to choose what is affirming for you. Try not to let fear be your guide. Choose what you think is best and let God do the rest.

TIP #14

MONEY BUYS CHOICES

The world is struggling to recover from an economic slowdown which has affected us all. The price of food and fuel is escalating, and in some countries unemployment has reached an all-time high. Many of us are surviving from pay cheque to pay cheque. We wonder what we, as individuals, can do to help ourselves through this time, and get out of the financial mess we may find ourselves in. I am no financial guru, but I would like to share some of my experiences and opinions with you.

We begin by looking at Want versus Need. Our basic needs are food, shelter and love. We all know that money won't buy love.

One day I was looking through the Canadian Tire flyer filled with pages of things I would like to have, such as new pots and pans, a reel to wind up my hose or a patio set for my deck, but I don't need them to improve my quality of life.

At one time or another, as most of us have had happen, I allowed my credit card to get away on me and am trying to pay it off. On my last statement was the comment that if I only make the minimum payment, my debt will be paid off in twenty three years. My interest rate is nineteen percent. *I work hard for my money, so why do I willingly give away nineteen cents of every dollar to a credit card company?* Good question.

Lately, I have found myself passing along some of the money management tips that I learned through the years to my daughter and oldest grandson. If you don't mind, I will share them with you.

When we bought our house the interest rate was twelve percent. At the time rates were fluid, some fluctuating as high as twenty five percent. First of all we got bi-weekly payments which meant several times a year, based on the number of Fridays in a month, we made an extra payment. I opened a separate savings account, and on payday would put the house payment plus an extra twenty dollars into this account. Every two weeks the bank took its money out, and I had a little extra. Over time the funds for the extra payments were there and I didn't have to worry whether there was enough or where the money was going to come from. Depending upon your mortgage contract, a lump sum payment of a few dollars once a year will save you thousands in the end.

Pay yourself first. Once again set up a savings account and have the bank automatically transfer a small sum into it each payday. The gurus say we should put aside ten percent, but that's not always possible. Let's say you begin with fifty dollars a month. In one year you will have six hundred dollars plus the interest the bank has paid you. Then the magic of compound interest cuts in. At the end of the next year, the bank will pay you interest on the interest they gave you in the previous year. There are financial tables available that demonstrate how this works, and when, at a given interest rate, your money will double.

Many years ago we were overwhelmed with credit card debit. If I remember correctly we had sixteen cards. Credit was easy to get, and with Bob away most of the time, we had to have some way to live. We never had any money because we had so many payments. About this same time I took a basic Book keeping course for our business, and one of the modules was about getting out of debt.

The teacher told us to take the credit card with the lowest balance and send more than the minimum payment each month. Continue paying the minimum balances on any other credit cards you may owe on. When the first card was paid off, take the money you are already paying out and add this to the minimum payment on the next card with the lowest balance. When those two are paid off, apply all of that money plus the minimum to the next and so on. Cut the cards up.

Today we only need one, perhaps two, so keep what you need and get rid of the rest. You know something, this works. Within two years we managed to pay off all of our balances and keep our future credit in good standing. Now, if we use these cards, we pay what we charged that month plus the minimum payment if we are carrying a balance. If you are paying your credit cards in full each month you are using somebody else's money for a short period of time with no finance charges. To me that's a good deal.

We kept two cards for the simple fact that when a person is travelling many motels are reluctant to accept cash. If there are damages to your room they want to be able to charge the repairs to your card. Keep in mind that you are also free to dispute these charges if you don't agree with them. They need to be able to prove what was done and that you are responsible for the damage.

As Canadians we thrive on plastic. Did you know that we are one of the highest users of debit cards in North America? Long ago we paid with cash or cheque. Of course, now merchants gladly accept plastic over paper because there are no NSF cheques they have to collect on. Each merchant pays a fee for each debit and credit card used in their place of business. I was surprised to learn that the credit cards with special advantages, such as air miles, costs the merchants more, and this cost is then passed along to us. The credit card company makes money both ways, charging the merchant and charging you interest if there is a balance carried over.

My oldest grandson has a very good job. The money he earns goes into his account as a direct deposit, and he uses his debit card exclusively. He has no concept about money. He is physically unaware of how much he is making and how much he is spending. As long as the card works, there is still money in the bank.

I confess there have been times when I have felt the same way, as long as the card still works I shop. If I have cash in my pocket I am much more aware of what I am spending. I try to keep a few dollars in my purse so I don't have to use my card for a three or five dollar item. I also keep a few dollars tucked away in my wallet for emergencies.

The real value of money is that it provides choices. We get to choose where, and what we spend our money on. But, in order to provide ourselves with these choices, we first have to learn to stop and ask "do I need this, or do I simply want it?"

One thing that saddens me is the lack of personal responsibility many people have about their finances. I admit I am from the old school, and have old school thinking, but when we get into debt we have nobody to blame but ourselves. We need to try and understand the motivation behind why we spend like we do, and why we repeatedly allow ourselves to get caught in this situation.

For some, fancy houses, expensive cars, and lots of toys are prestige symbols that define who they are. My dad was raised in poverty on a native reserve. When he got older he had to have the best of everything; the three hundred dollar suit, and the top of the line car. This was his way of proving to himself that his status in the world had improved, and that he was no longer that poor hungry child. My mom had to find a way to clothe and feed seven children on what was left. He didn't deliberately intend for his family to do without, but his emotional needs were far greater than he could comprehend.

Many caught up in this situation live in constant fear of losing what they have. Their self-worth is tied up in proving to the world that they deserve all of the trappings. I know that this doesn't make them any happier than you or I who may have less.

Last week I was looking after my younger three grandsons. Their mom was working days and this meant they arrive early in the morning and I give them supper. The first day Tyler asked if his little friend could stay and eat with us. That little boy was hungry, eventually cleaning up all of the left overs. The next day we ate earlier, and at our usual supper time Tyler's friend knocked on the door wondering if we had eaten yet. He was hungry, and there was nobody home to feed him. He is eight years old, in grade three and literally raising himself. He is lonely and extremely vulnerable, attaching himself to whoever will play with him and possibly give him something to eat.

Both of his parents work late. I don't know who they are, or their financial circumstance, but I do know their child came to my door asking to be fed. All of the money in the world isn't going to give this little boy what he needs. The saddest part is that he isn't an exception; this goes on in our towns and cities all the time. My question is, what does this say about us? Do we have our priorities straight?

Money buys choices, but credit and credit cards enslave us. Essentially, we spend our lives working for someone else. The houses, vehicles, toys soon need to be replaced or have become outdated. We are encouraged to buy bigger and better. We have to choose what is important to us. Do we really need the fifty inch Television set we may still be paying for three years down the road?

I do know one thing for sure, a fancy house isn't going to put its arms around you and say "I love you." Good stewardship of our finances allows us to have both.

As an afterthought, one of the facts that has held true throughout the years is that women are at a financial disadvantage. We are still only making eighty three cents of a man's dollar, and most of our work is at the lower end of the pay scale.

This disparity shows up at retirement. A friend of mine worked all of her life, taking time off to have her children, and then going back to work. When she applied for her Canadian Pension Plan benefits, she received twenty five percent of her husband's rates. Instead of retiring she had no choice but to keep on working for a couple more years.. Even though they had been doing the same work the last few years ,she received less than him. Many of her previous jobs had been at the lower end of the pay scale, and her total contributions had been less.

This is a reality for many people, especially those self-employed. If I had a do over, I would make saving money for my retirement a priority or make sure I worked for a company with a good retirement plan.

TIP #15

BIG ME - little me

I looked inside my mind
to see what I could find;
Was I surprised to see
A "spirit' called "BIG ME."

Full of courage, faith and love
A gift for sure from one above.
It said "You can, you will, you must,
All is yours if you'll just trust.

Big me says, "You can do it, charge ahead
You have the strength – there's nothing to dread.
Day by day, just do your task
It's all so simple if you'll just "Ask."

Filled with energy, vitality and hope
With all my trials, I now can cope.
Victory is mine, I'll claim the cup!
Nothing will stop me! I'm on my way up!

Then something appeared at the side of my mind,
From the corner came feelings of another kind.
A horrible creature called "Little me"
Reared its ugly head for all to see.

Little me is unsure, full of doubt and fears,
"You can't do it," it always cheers.
It wants me to walk on the downbeat side,
Dark emotions of guilt are its pride.

So now I'm confused, which shall I follow?
Little me says "be jealous, be hollow."
Do you really believe <u>you</u> can be great?
It's in control when I'm filled with hate.

Then I stamp my foot, and take a stand
I choose "Big Me" to lend a hand.
I'll do my work and reap the reward,
Negative thinking I can't afford.

"Little me" – "Big Me" will always be inside
To which do I have power to be my guide?
They will struggle, but the choice is mine.
I'll pick "Big Me" and I'll be fine.

As long as I know that every day
Little me will want to act out its play.
I'll just relax and say "It's O.K.
I know you have come but you can't stay."

"Big Me" is my special friend
I choose to walk with her to the end.
I pray each day with thanks and love
For this "BIG ME"- my gift from above.

Author Unknown

TIP #16

WHAT ARE YOU TOLERATING?

Every once in a while Jennie would ask me the question "what are you tolerating?" What thoughts or actions was I putting up with that I didn't approve of? Every time she brought this up I side stepped her question because I didn't want to answer it.

Why? Because, if I answered her question, then I knew I would have face up to the situation, then feel compelled to do something I didn't want to. In this case I was hoping that ignorance was bliss.

Let me see, what am I tolerating besides not being able to get something done until I have asked three or four times, the toilet paper not being put on the roller thing or the cap being left off the toothpaste? I could go on and on, but I'm sure you have a few zingers of your own you could add to my list.

Sometimes I gave up. I got tired of waiting for what I asked for to happen. One day I realized this had become a pattern that my family and I had fallen into it. I would ask, and then wait for action. This was hard because I am the kind of person who wants things done right now, not later. In the end I gave up expecting what I wanted to be done for me.

When I reached the end of my patience I adopted the attitude of "I will do it myself." Jennie would tell me to ask again for what I wanted, but I found that hard to do because I thought once should be enough. I also learned that if I said "at your convenience" weeks could pass before anyone got around to it. I was frustrated most of the time.

Somewhere along the line, I learned to settle for what I received, not what I wanted. It didn't matter whether I was happy or not, I was getting what I deserved. I didn't make a fuss because that might lead to confrontation.

Nobody can read our minds. If we want something to change, we have to make our request known in such a way that the other person understands that we expect action in return, preferably one that makes us happy. Believe me, once the pattern of "if I wait long enough she will eventually stop asking" is established it's hard to break. This is about having respect for each other.

You have to decide for yourself if what you are tolerating is worth the hassle or not. If you don't ask, you don't get. If we want respect, we have to ask that we be treated respectfully.

In some relationships control becomes a factor. Who is going to win the argument? Who is going to be the boss? Often, many of these relationships fail to learn the art of compromise or working together.

So, I ask you what are you tolerating and why? You decide if the issue needs to be addressed. If so, ask for what you want. If not, let it go. If this isn't the right time, deal with the issue at a later date, but don't ignore it completely. You don't need to go around feeling as if nobody is listening to you all the time.

One more question – what are you tolerating about yourself that makes you unhappy? I know that for my health to improve I should lose some weight. Do I do anything about it? No! I want to get up one morning, look in the mirror, and see that magically I have lost twenty pounds, but we both know that isn't going to happen. So now what? Either I stop worrying or do something to take the extra pounds off.

In reality this is a big question. What do you consistently put yourself down about, ignore or put off. Is there something you know you should do, but don't for whatever reason? Without being self-critical, acknowledge what you are tolerating. Now try to understand what is behind your thinking. Why are you putting up with this? Is there anything you can do?

Next it's decision time. You have a choice, you can choose to do what you have to, or you can let things remain the same as they are. It's entirely up to you because you are the one who has to live with the consequences of your decision.

The magic word is choice - what are you going to do? This choice isn't about determining who is right or who is wrong. The question is, are you willing to continue tolerating what is bothering you, or are you going to decide it's not that big of a deal and let it go?

We also have to understand that we can't make others do something if they don't want to. Most will begrudge us every minute it takes. One way to get around this is to make the other person part of the decision making process. "Is there any way you could.......?" When they decide to respond it will be because they choose to, not because they feel they have to. Now they have ownership in the process.

This is a two way street. Believe it or not, there are things or actions that other people are barely tolerating about us. When this is brought to our attention, we need to be receptive to what they are saying, whether we agree or not, and we most likely won't

Perhaps there is a creative solution. Rather than argue about the cap being off the toothpaste maybe you could each have your own tube. If you want the cap on yours that's fine, if the other person leaves the cap off his/hers, that's up to them.

This may or may not work the first few times you try it, but it's important that you begin to do something about what you are tolerating. Deciding that you will no longer tolerate a certain behavior means you've the taken the first in a series of actions about facing the issue, That's what is important, now you can follow up to the best of your ability. Bravo, good for you! If you can do this once, you can do it the next time and the next. There is no stopping you now.

TIP #17

STAND UP FOR WHAT YOU BELIEVE IN

As I mature I think differently about many things. I realize I have lived the largest part of my life, and the time I have left is gradually getting shorter. I am less tolerant of all of the crap that goes on between people and in this world. I am learning to live and let live.

In order to grow, we have to make mistakes, take risks, have multiple failures and successes, experience hurt and love. We lose people we care for, but also welcome others and experience the joy they bring with them.

One of my dreams was to write a book which I accomplished in 2009. I experienced the most awesome feeling in the world when I opened open the box and saw all of the books with my name on the front. I giggled and danced around my kitchen. This was mine. I did this.

A year later, I sent my book to an editor in California, whom I thought, would be able to help me get it published. Everything was wrong; the cover, the setup, the print was too big and the book was grammatically incorrect. I was devastated. Some of the fixes were easy, but following some of her suggestions meant I would lose my voice. The words in the book would no longer be the perfect ones I wanted to say. She didn't understand what I was trying to do.

"This looks and reads like a self-published book." I was told.

"Yes it does, "I replied to her "because it is. This is my

story, my book and my way of writing. If I make the changes you are suggesting, I will lose some of the importance of what I am trying to say."

I made the choice of leaving everything the way it was. I stood up for the message I wanted to convey. So what if it doesn't meet all of the literary standards, my book, as written, is reaching out and touching people's lives.

There comes a time when we need to stand up for what we want and for what we believe in. It doesn't matter whether we are right or wrong, we need to have the courage of our convictions. At first we may only be one voice, but when we look into history Gandhi, Nelson Mandela, and John F Kennedy were only one voice yet look at the differences they made in this world. They challenged us to think and evaluate what was possible. Look at what Terry Fox accomplished by being only one person and attempting to run across Canada. The money raised is to be used for Cancer research, and the odds of survival are improving.

In the years 1968 -1969 those of us who graduated as Laboratory and X-Ray Technicians thought that we needed a voice in developing our wage and employment agreements with the government. Wages and working conditions were inconsistent across the province. We formed a Society; ASCLXT, the Alberta Society for Certified Laboratory and X-ray Technicians, and in 1971, two of us negotiated our first contract with the Provincial government. Later I worked with our group and another which eventually led to several more groups amalgamating with us to form Health Sciences Association of Alberta, which currently represents two hundred and fifty health care groups in the province. The Health care workers in Saskatchewan and British Columbia have adopted our format to set up similar Health Sciences Association in their own provinces. This is an example of what one voice joining with another, who believed in the same thing, can accomplish.

When you speak up you become powerful. You become a voice to be reckoned with. Vocal minorities can become majorities when enough voices unite in a common cause. Your strength comes from what you believe in and are passionate about.

We must determine for ourselves if our cause is for the common good or is it self-serving. Years ago I sat as a Trustee on our local Catholic School board. Intimidation and harassment were a fact of life. Frequently we had to make unpopular decisions based upon what was fair to the district, not one that only served a specific group.

Often I would pray to be shown the best way and voted as I saw fit. When a group came forward with an idea, they always had my deepest admiration, but too many times the ideas were self-serving. These exchanges frequently became bitter, and the attacks personal. Most of the time, the ideas were excellent and provided us with a concept of a better way of running the schools and improving the quality of education for the children. Because these groups spoke up, they made a difference for all of the children in the district.

I am only one voice in the wilderness, but I am determined to be heard. There will always be nay Sayers who will go to extremes to dominate and silence us. Don't let that stop you. If you have the courage of your convictions, somebody will hear you. Speak up and let people know what you think. Our silence dooms us, forcing us to go along with what others are thinking or saying. If we want or need something different in our lives, we have to make our voices heard.

TIP #18

PICK YOUR BATTLES

A very wise man once told me, "Pick your battles. Fight for what is important. Save your energy for the things that really matter." Thank you, Walt Elliott. We miss you! You were a good friend and neighbor.

These words are so true. We can't win every battle we fight. I believe this is especially true when it comes to our children. Of course we want them to obey us; we want them to have high morals and standards. We want them to stay away from drugs and booze, but if we fight them every inch of the way over the small things, it's very possible we will lose on the big things too.

As parents we have to decide what is important to us. Do we scream and holler and create a big scene because the little darlings don't take the garbage out when they were told to, or if their music is too loud? Isn't it better to save this energy until we discover our twelve year old is smoking pot and sexually active?

Our kids test us all the time. I used to think that when they became adults this would stop, but it doesn't. My mom used to say, "Little kids, little problems - big kids, big problems." Today I understand what she was talking about. No matter how old they are, we never stop worrying about them.

We need to be firm in our priorities, and establish what is acceptable or unacceptable to us. When we establish boundaries, our children learn to function within them. I refuse to allow a certain swear word to be uttered in my house. My children and husband know that, and although they slip once in a while, they don't talk that way around me, but I can't control how they talk outside of my home. They have been taught better.

Eventually, I learned how to judge what was important and what was not. I learned to ask myself "is this going to matter in five months or five years from now?" In five years will it matter that junior was slow taking the garbage out? In the whole scheme of life is it that important? If little Suzie is smoking pot now what could that mean in five years? What can I do today that will make a difference?

I value those teachable moments with my grandchildren when we have an opportunity to discuss what is right and wrong. If I repeat the same message often enough, I hope they will eventually understand what I am trying to say.

Now that my children are grown and have families of their own I count my lucky stars. There were times when their lives could have gone either way. The things we had to deal with as a family were nothing compared to what other families faced. I am very proud of them today.

To tell you the truth, I'm also enjoying those sweet moments I call revenge. My one grandson is as outspoken and confident as his mother was at the same age. She was a handful, and so is he. I smile sweetly when she is frustrated and tell her "now you know what it was like raising you." For some strange reason she doesn't appreciate my comment, or my sense of humor.

I wasn't very good with the "tough love" policy. One time a neighbor's fourteen year old grandson ran away from his parents. They had moved to southern Alberta and he didn't want to be there, so he hitchhiked back up north. My kids found him and brought him home like a stray kitten. I notified his parents and grandparents so they knew where he was, and that he was safe.

He stayed with us for several weeks until the day his mother phoned and insisted I ask him to leave. She told me that he would never come home as long as he was safe and comfortable. She was absolutely right.

I called him upstairs, and told him he would have to leave in the morning. This was one of the hardest things I have ever had to do in my life. I cried as he angrily stormed out the door. I was ravaged with guilt when I heard he was sleeping in the post office to stay warm. Eventually he went home. Today he is a fine young man with a family of his own and a good job. I honestly don't know if he has ever forgiven me, but I know that five years later my actions made a difference.

At one time there was a book titled *"Don't Sweat the Small Stuff"* written by Richard Carlson. Can you agree with me when I say the little things we fret about on a daily basis are the ones that get us down? The toilet seat left up, the cap off the tooth paste, and dirty clothes beside the hamper irritate us to no end, but are they really important? The trouble with these irritations is that they tend to become more important than they really are. They begin to fester, one thing leads to another, the anger builds until there is a blow up. Marriages and relationships often end over the little things.

Save your energy for the big battles. If some small annoyance is getting in your way, speak up. Tell others what you want, ask for what you need. Don't let trivial things overwhelm you and become more important than they are. Ask yourself, "is this going to matter in five months or five years from now?" To me what matters most is how we spend our time with others. Five years from now that will have made the biggest difference.

TIP #19

LIVE IN YOUR PERSONAL POWER

Recently I read a book called "Tears in the Desert" by Hamila Bashir and with Damien Lewis. This is a true story about a young black woman born in Darfur Africa who left home, and went to college to become a doctor. While there, the war with the Arabs broke out. She was sent to a large hospital to complete her training, and considered treating the black rebels as well as the influential Arabs as part of her duty.

She was reported to the police by a fellow employee, taken away, threatened, and interrogated. As punishment she was removed from that hospital before completing her training, and sent to a community in a distant area of the country. The war was also encroaching on this area, and after clinic hours she would secretly treat the wounded rebels, often sending first aid packages and medicine home with them. Once again, the police spied on her every move.

One day a group of Arab soldiers forced their way into the local girls school and gang raped forty young girls between the ages of seven and thirteen years. The parents could hear their daughters screaming, but the army held them back at gun point until the soldiers were finished. Because she was the only doctor available, most of the girls were brought to her. This is a country that believes in female circumcision, and many of these young girls had been literally torn apart, and needed to be sewn back together. The belief behind this horrific act was that a female is soiled if she has intercourse before marriage, and no man will want her. The proliferation of children would be stopped.

When an investigative team from the United Nations approached the doctor to find out the truth about the attack she supplied what they needed. Several days later officers of the Arab army kidnapped her from the clinic to punish her for helping the rebels and speaking to the U N. They confined her in a shed on their base, interrogated, and gang raped her for five day before letting her go. She was allowed to live because now she was also worthless.

She left that area, and after a journey fraught with danger, she found her way back to her own village and family. Eventually the war arrived there as well. A gunship helicopter strafed her village, killing most of the inhabitants including her father and grandmother. Her mother and little sister escaped into the hills, and she never saw them again.

The story continues as she escapes to England where she marries a childhood acquaintance and becomes "the voice for the women of Darfur," publicly speaking out about the tragedy engulfing the women of her country.

When I finished this book I was upset and angry. The intimidation, the rapes were about control. We experience a feeling of powerlessness when others think they have authority over our body and our life.

As I was discussing this book with my coach she helped me realize I was angry because that's how I have felt most of my life. Everything I had done up until now was about trying to cope and please those I felt had control over me.

As I grew stronger, I began to develop a sense of who I was. I began to take my independence back. Now I know I always had a choice about what was going on, but

I didn't understand that before. I also began to understand that the basis of my fear came from thinking I had no control over my life.

I remember asking myself at the time *"was I strong enough? Was I capable of looking after myself and my children? Could I? Would I? Should I?"* I didn't trust my own thinking because after all, I was getting what I deserved.

I have since realized that I gave my power away in order to keep peace and avoid conflict, thus allowing others to make my decisions for me. Naturally their decisions concerned what was best for them, and they didn't need to be accountable. The one thing I know for sure is that feeling powerless undermines our ability to think and do for ourselves.

The remote control for the TV set is always a good illustration. Whoever has the remote, controls the programming! When our oldest grandson was small, he would turn the TV to his programs then hide the remote so that his poppa couldn't have it. You wouldn't believe the kerfuffle that went into searching for the darned thing. Sometimes peace wasn't restored until my husband phoned our grandson to find out where it was hidden. There were times I wasn't sure who was the child and who was the adult.

That struggle, however small, was about power. Rape, child and spousal abuse is all about power, and as long as we are afraid to take matters into our own hands and change the situation, we remain powerless. Our personal power comes when we begin deciding what is best for us, making our own choices and striving for independence in our thinking and actions.

There are other things that make us feel powerless. Many times we are at the mercy of another's opinion. A young couple I know wanted to build a new house. They saved some money, and sold their current home for a good price. They went to the bank, their loan was approved, the plans were drawn up, and the builder was hired. Then the bank asked them to bring the plans back for an appraisal, which of course, they had to pay for. Then, before the loan would be granted again, they were informed that they had to provide another twenty five thousand dollars in cash. How many of us have that kind of money sitting around?

Fortunately they were able to buy a house, but it wasn't what they wanted. In this case they had no control over what was happening, and were forced into an uncomfortable situation not of their own making. I don't pretend to know all of the ins and outs of the deal, but I do know they felt powerless and angry.

These types of situations happen to all of us, and contribute to our feeling that others have more control over our lives than we do. We often end up wondering why we even bothered in the first place.

Our work environment can also make us feel powerless, and no matter how hard we try, whatever we do is wrong. We are at the mercy of our supervisors who may pass on their projects with impossible deadlines, then blame us when they are not completed. Maybe the attitude is "my way or the highway. If you don't want this job I can easily find someone who does."

One of the things I have recently become acquainted with is work place bullying, and how prevalent it is in our society. Definition time - a bully is a person who teases, frightens or hurts people they perceive to be smaller or weaker.

This can come in the form of sexual or sexual harassment, threats about job security and so on. The person being harassed feels defenseless, and that they are at the mercy of the other person. The bully finds a weak spot in the personality or character of another then uses this as weapon to manipulate them.

Often we find these same people are feeling a loss of power in their own lives, and exercising a form of control over others is a way of making themselves feel better. Many times, even though we resent their treatment, we comply because we feel that we have no other choice.

The bottom line is that we, as a consumer, a person, a spouse, must begin to understand that each of us has the power to change our own lives. In essence I am saying that "I'm as mad as hell and I'm not going to take this anymore." I'm striving to take back the power over my own life, and I hope you will find the courage to do the same.

To my daughters I say "you decide what you want and then do and then do whatever is necessary. Be in charge of your own life. Walk away from people who are trying to control your thoughts and actions. Be independent in your thinking. If something is important to you, then do whatever you have to for your own reasons."

When we are in harmony with our values, choices and decisions, we walk in our personal power. When we do what is best for us, our feelings of powerlessness disappear. We begin to come into our own.

One battle doesn't win a war, but each tiny victory helps determine the outcome.

TIP #20

EMPOWER YOURSELF

Today I had one of those light bulb moments. I realized something for the first time, and then asked myself how come I didn't know this before?

I realized there are two types of people on this earth. There are those who say no and mean it, then the rest of us. I am one of the latter, an enabler. I accept other people's excuses for their self-destructive behavior, and by doing so, allow them to continue. I don't hold them accountable or responsible for their own actions. I accept their behavior because this is easier than confronting them. I wasn't born yesterday, and these people aren't really fooling me, they simply think they are. Have you ever found yourself in this same position?

Often, instead of demanding answers, we justify their actions by saying "what goes around comes around, and they have to live with their conscience."

During my light bulb moment, I realized I was doing exactly the same thing with my own children, and it had to stop. I realized that I wasn't helping, and in some ways, I was actually holding them back. I was taking responsibility for their problems instead of letting them figure them out for themselves.

The question became, how do I make them accountable, hold them true to their word, on an adult to adult basis, without sounding like I was telling them what to do? I want my children to be as independent as possible, and make their own decisions whether I agree with them or not.

I thought about this for a long time then the answer came to me. All I had to do was ask the question "what do you think you should do?" When they answered this question they began taking ownership of the solution. They became more willing to think out, and then follow their own course of action. The hardest part, once I asked this question, was keeping my mouth shut, and letting them follow through on their decision. This was especially hard when I didn't agree. I had to keep reminding myself they are doing what is best for them. My role became saying to them "I will support you in any decision you make."

We teach people how to treat us. If we teach others to depend upon us to solve their problems, they'll let us take the lead. They will expect us to bail them out every time something goes wrong. It's our own fault because we have given them the right to expect this. If we allow others to treat us with disrespect, we are teaching them to disrespect us. I have been forced to say to my grandchildren "this is my house. When you are here you will treat this place and me with respect." They don't like it, but sometimes they need to be reminded.

On the other hand, when we insist upon others doing what we tell them, we are treating them disrespectfully and taking their power away, Empowerment is a two-fold process – a giver and a taker. We forget that we don't have to live with the consequences of the decision; we get to walk away if we are wrong

My point is that subconsciously we allow or even encourage these patterns to continue because they have always been that way. We fail to take the necessary action that will make things different. At some point, we need to have enough confidence to stand and declare enough is enough. We need to learn to say "no" and mean what we say.

When we empower ourselves, we begin teaching others what is acceptable to us and what isn't. They'll continue to test us, but if we stand firm, and continue telling them what we want, they will eventually learn. The secret is to make them think this is their own idea.

I have been rambling a bit so back to "the question." When people reach their own conclusions or decisions, they are more willing to follow through. We are empowering them to take control and think for themselves. I have found that they will eagerly inform you about what they think they should do, and already have the correct solution. They merely need reassurance.

Before I leave you, I have one more thought. As we grow older there are many people, especially our adult children, who think they know what's best for us. Remember that you have a voice, that you are still capable of making your own decisions. I have seen cases where the children think they know what is best for the parent, and push their own agenda without considering what the parents want or wish for. If you feel you are in this situation remember you still have the right to be heard. Speak up if you feel uncomfortable or feel like you are being forced into something you don't want.

Many times I have heard older people say "I don't want to go live in a lodge." Find out their reasoning, their fears and give this valid consideration A few years ago I helped with a survey by interviewing the seniors in our community about where they would prefer to live. Each one of them wanted to stay in their home and be independent until it was no longer possible, then they would move to a facility to wait until they died. This really made me stop and think.

Our idea of living in a facility, such as a lodge is totally different than theirs. We think that it's a good place to go. Their meals are looked after, there are other people to communicate with, and they have a stable environment. To some of the people I spoke with moving into a lodge meant a loss of their independence, and their usefulness to society. Some even thought their families would give up on them, and stay away.

As adult children we still need to listen to our parents. The difference is now we need to learn to listen for what is being said, rather than telling them what we think they are saying. I know this seems foolish, but our parents have lived much longer than we have, and probably have questions or valid reasons behind their thinking. Even if their body is old and frail, that doesn't mean their mind is old and frail also.

Empower them, if possible, by giving them a say in any decision-making process involving their well-being. Co-operation works miracles.

TIP #21

<u>Strength and Courage</u>

It takes strength to be certain. It takes courage to have doubts.
It takes strength to fit in. It takes courage to stand out.
It takes strength to share a friend's pain. It takes courage to
feel your own pain
.It takes strength to hide your own pain. It takes courage to
show it and deal with it.
It takes strength to stand guard. It takes courage to let down
your guard.
It takes strength to conquer. It takes courage to surrender.
It takes strength to embrace abuses. It takes courage to stop
them.
It takes strength to stand alone. It takes courage to lean on a
friend.
It takes strength to love. It takes courage to be loved.
It takes strength to survive. It takes courage to live.
May you find strength and courage in everything you do
and may your life be filled with Friendship and Love!

Communicator/ Hyena Review

Sept . 24 issue, 20002

Tip #22

BOUNDARIES

One positive thing about starting over is that we get to set new boundaries for ourselves and for others. To quote Ann Vertel from her e-zine, *"boundaries are your invisible property lines that define who you are and protect you from the unacceptable behavior of others. You must communicate those boundaries to others. The goal is to have others change their unacceptable behavior when they are around you."*

(www.AnnVertel.com)

I like to feel needed, to feel that I am making a contribution, and that I am making a difference. At one time I would go overboard to feel accepted. I yearned for the confirmation that what I was doing was "good."

When my daughter and her husband split up I faced a very real internal struggle. A part of me wanted to take her and her children under my care. I wanted to love them, protect them from the hurt, and to literally step in and take over.

The other part of me said, "No, I can't do that. This is a long term situation, and she needs to be able to do this for herself. She is going to be a single parent for a long time."

In the end, I set a boundary. I told her "I will love and support you. I will help you with the kids when I am needed. I will give them breakfast and supper when you are working days, but I want to be their grandmother, not their primary care giver."

Please understand, these boundaries were for me, not for her. This way I wasn't consumed by all the drama going on in her life. Instead of trying to fix everything, I gave her the freedom to follow her own path.

Boundaries are also the self-imposed limits of what we will or will not do, or what kind of treatment we will accept from others. Remember, we teach people how to treat us by not speaking up or letting them know what is or isn't appropriate.

Let's say you left a relationship because it was verbally abusive. "How can you be so stupid? Can't you get anything right" and so on. Then you meet somebody new that you care for. At first everything is wonderful, and then the snide remarks begin. This is your opportunity to set that new boundary "I am not willing to stay in this relationship if you continue speaking to me that way. I feel you are being disrespectful."

Maybe there are times when you have to say, "I am a grown mature woman quite capable of looking after myself. Although you may disagree with my decision, this is the right one for me at this time."

Now others know how much you are willing to take. If the line is crossed, then you have the choice of leaving or continuing the relationship. If you don't set some sort of boundary at the beginning, then it becomes nearly impossible later on, the other person will continue saying and doing whatever they please

We know ourselves better than anyone else. If we reach the point where we feel we are being taken advantage of, we always have the choice of allowing it to continue or putting a stop to it.

Each of us has the ability to set a limit on what we are willing to accept. When that limit is exceeded we need to take a step back, and ask ourselves "what do I want? What is best for me in this situation?" Before these limits have been exceeded, we need to step up and speak out.

I love my grandchildren. I love spending time and doing things with them. At first I enjoyed being asked to look after the boys and I always said yes, but after a while, I began to feel a twinge of resentment. By always making myself available I was teaching my children that they didn't have to consider that I may have things to do that were important to me. I couldn't always put my plans on the back burner as I had been doing.

Finally I learned to say, "No, I can't today because I have a meeting, or I can take them for the morning but not in the afternoon."

Continually saying yes wasn't doing either of us any favors. When I established a boundary they learned to solve their own dilemma, and I am happy to say our relationship greatly improved. We developed the unspoken agreement that I would if I could, but if not, they were willing to look elsewhere. We all learned a valuable lesson from this experience.

Setting new boundaries means I am saying to my daughter, "you are a strong capable woman who can make the best of this situation for you and your family. I am here, if and when you need my support, but you can get through this difficult time."

I'm also acknowledging to myself that I have taught her well and that I believe in her and her abilities. I can sit back and support her, knowing she will handle this breakup the best way she sees fit.

This was an important growth step for me. I empowered myself by stating limits which was something I had never done before. At first I felt very guilty. She needs me, I should be there, but this way is healthier mentally and emotionally for both of us. Like any other mother, I don't always agree with what my children are doing, but I try to respect their decisions.

TIP #23

THE NEED TO BE NEEDED

Based upon my own experiences, the best tip I can offer is that if you want to feel needed get a puppy. Having a dog will save you a whole lot of grief and loss of self-confidence. You may not think much of my idea, but let's take a look at it.

A puppy is a baby that needs to be fed, watered, cleaned up behind, and groomed. This little creature can barely fend for itself, and at first is dependent upon us for its wellbeing. Of course, after it works its way into our heart, this creature takes over and thinks it's the boss. But in the meantime, we get to lavish our time and attention on it, and in turn receive unconditional love. There is no hidden agenda, and no matter what happens, it greets us with its wagging tail, licks our face and appreciates us for who we are. This puppy will listen to our tales of woe or when we cry. It will treat us respectfully when we open our hearts and speak our truth.

During the period of time my husband worked away from home, I was often lonely. I kept myself busy, but I needed something else alive in my house. I had a disdainful cat that was available when she wanted to be, and on her terms.

One day I met one of my clients in the drug store and she was telling me about these cute little puppies she had for sale. During the course of our conversation I mentioned that I would like to have another dog but Bob was opposed to the idea. One animal was enough. After I got home, she called and asked if I would be willing to make a trade, a puppy for some of my products. By the end of that afternoon, I was in possession of Snoopy, a cute fluffy white dog with three black spots on its back.

Now I had another problem. Bob had decreed there were to be no more dogs, and of course, I listened to everything he said. Earlier in the day I had splurged and bought a new dishwasher after years of going without.

That evening he phoned as usual, to see how things were at home and I said to him "Guess what? I bought a new dishwasher today, and when they delivered it there was a puppy inside."

"Was it alive?" he asked.

"Yes. I guess they were giving away free puppies with purchase."

There was dead silence on the phone. Ironically he was calling to tell me that he found a Shih Tzu in a nearby town that he was thinking of buying.. Great minds really do think alike. Needless to say Snoopy livened up our house, and kept me busy cleaning up behind him, and rescuing my shoes. Definitely his presence added to my quality of life.

When I look back at that needy phase of my life, I was feeling unfulfilled as a person. My business wasn't doing as well as I wanted it to. My life lacked urgency, didn't feel important, and didn't seem to have the same value as before. Most of all, I didn't feel valued as a person. Going out of my way to do little things for people so they would appreciate me became my drug of choice. I needed my fix to prove I was good enough.

When we are seeking approval we don't feel deserving

of the nice things being said to us. This was an oxymoron. I was seeking approval, yet when I got what I was looking for, I couldn't accept it, because I felt I wasn't deserving. You figure that out.

I lost who I was. My purpose in life and for work was unclear. No matter how hard I tried, I couldn't get the approval and respect from the people I most wanted it to come from.

After losing my mother to cancer and being rejected by my brothers and sisters, I internalized my deep pain. My husband, children and friends supported me, but I struggled to get past my overpowering feeling of loss.

I needed to be needed, to feel wanted, to be respected, and to make my soul realize I was a good person. Most of all, I longed for what would never be, a part of the lives of my brothers and sisters. I wanted to be embraced, and welcomed back into the family fold.

After many years of trying I finally gave up. I was learning to recognize who I was and what I stood for. Even now, fourteen years later, I still don't understand what happened.

Only now am I realizing this wasn't about me. This whole situation was about them and their personal feelings, and that I hadn't done anything wrong. I have learned to accept the situation as it is, and now I know there is nothing more I can do. The solution is not in my hands. I pray for them, hope they have good lives, and that maybe one day....... I look upon my children and grandchildren and thank God for them every day.

I am truly grateful for my blessings and for what I have been given. Through this experience, I learned that I already possess everything I need. You too have everything you need in your life. All we have to do is seek and find it within ourselves and stop looking to outside forces to make us happy. Happiness really is an inside job!

TIP #24

DEFINING MOMENTS

"There is a definitive moment we use as a reference because they break our sense of continuity; they change the direction of time. We can look at these events and we can say of the things will never be the same again."

Margaret Atwood

Each of us has those defining moments, those instances or choices that alter our life forever. We end up going in a completely different direction than we planned. Some may seem trivial at the time, but ended up with huge consequences. Some were good, some not, but the culmination of these events shaped us into who we are today.

One for me was the morning I got off the bus to begin a one year posting as a Lab and x-ray Technician in the Village of Berwyn. My plan was to fulfill the requirements of my contract with the government, then go to Inuvik where a job was waiting for me. I planned on working very hard and completing my assignments in six months. Forty some years later I am still here.

Sometimes when I look back, I want to say *"I wish I knew then what I know now. I would have laughed more, worried less, had more fun and not been so serious."* What I didn't realize before is that things work out the way they are supposed to.

"Oh please" you say, "How can you believe that? I know my life would have been better if .... The truth is we don't know, and never will. We are feeding ourselves an illusion about what we think our life might have been. We are back to the "If only." Some people continue thinking this way for years; they torture themselves over their choices, and in the meantime, rob their todays of joy and happiness.

My mom was engaged to another man before she met my dad. It was war time and he was in the service. When the two sets of parents got together they couldn't get along, and eventually the two of them broke up. Within a short period of time she met my dad, whom her parents didn't particularly care for. I think they called him a rang-a-tang. Anyway they were total opposites.

More than once I heard my mom say, "I should have married Paul." Yet after my dad passed away I found her in the basement crying, and I have never forgotten her words. "I've not only lost my husband, I have lost my best friend."

I wasn't mature enough at the time to appreciate or truly understand what she was telling me. Today I realize she was saying that in spite of all the hardships their marriage endured, they were attuned to each other. This was more than love. It was a deeper understanding of what they meant to each other.

Because of their defining moment I was born, my children were born, and my grandchildren walk upon this earth. Was this not meant to be?

I am sure that if you think back, you will be able to see some defining moments in your own life. You are where you are supposed to be right now. That was the plan.

Many years ago we went to Hawaii with Bob's family. His sister, her husband and the two of us rented a car and were on our way to visit the Punch Bowl war memorial.

We missed our turn off, had to take the next one, and ended up in a residential area. Eventually we got where we were going, but we also got a glimpse of how the Hawaiian people lived. The moment when we missed our turn we were granted an opportunity to see and understand more than we would have other wise

We make our decisions or choices based on the information we have at the time. If we buy into the theory that our life is going the way it's meant to, then we need to learn to live in the now. That is all we have, this minute, this hour

A woman is told "we got all of the cancer." She has a choice, take a course of chemotherapy or do nothing. She chose to trust that her cancer truly was gone and does nothing. Two years later she is fighting for her life. Would it have made a difference? Maybe? Maybe not?

I hear people judging her saying that she made a mistake. If she had done what she should have in the first place, she wouldn't be in this situation now. She and her family made their decision based upon the information they were given at that time. It's always easier for us to judge others because we aren't walking in their shoes. Those who have battled cancer might say that she made the correct decision. None of us is right, and quite frankly, this is none of our business. She did what she thought was best.

What's done is done. We aren't born with a do over button. If we have a button, it's a repeat button. The important thing is that now, today, we make the best informed decision we can, and this will be one of our defining moments.

When we are honoring ourselves, we are attempting to do the best we can at that given moment. We have no idea what fate has in store for us.

Don't second guess yourself; all you will end up doing is driving yourself crazy. This is what was, this is what I chose to do, and now I accept my decision. There is no right or wrong because I believe our journey is predetermined, and we have much to look forward to along the way.

Be Strong! Do what is best for you at this time, and then move into your future with the knowledge and confidence that you are exactly where you are supposed to be. Everything that is going on in your life is for a reason. If things were truly meant to be different, the results would have been different.

Sometimes defining moments are not your choice – your spouse passes away, you are fired from your job, your husband announces that he wants a divorce. You are left asking why? What happened?

The first thing we do is blame ourselves – if I had done this or done that. We have all been there one time or another.

Be true to who you are and give yourself the time, the love and the support you need. More than ever you need to do what is best for you. Look after yourself mentally, physically and spiritually. Give yourself permission to inch your way forward. If we stay mired in our tears, we remain stuck. Life moves on without us.

No, this wasn't your choice, your decision. This isn't what you want, but remember there is no do over button. Each of us, through trial, and mostly error find the path again. Try to remember that your guide is doing what is best for you, at this time, and under these circumstances. Make your decision and then move on.

Sometimes the worst events we encounter in our life prepare us for the wonderful things that are to come in our future. No matter what we may guess, we have no way of actually knowing until we are there. Trust your instincts. Trust yourself. Let go of what was, or what could have been, and step boldly into your future.

TIP #25

EVERYTHING IS ON THE OTHER SIDE OF FEAR

Sometimes I feel that I have been afraid of something my whole life - that I would say or do something wrong or make a fool of myself. I assume there have been times some of you have felt the same way.

What is fear really? One explanation I was taught is that fear is False Expectations Appearing Real. Good old Funk and Wagnall tell us that fear is an anxious or uneasy feeling, to perceive a threat. To be afraid is to be in a mental state which may have a real or imagined course, and may last for a long or short time.

I am afraid of heights. I tell myself that anything higher than me is too high. Even to stand on a chair to reach into the top cupboard gives me that queasy feeling in my tummy, and I am thinking "*what if I fall?*" I have carried this to extremes. One time I went to Edmonton with the grade nine class, and we toured the TELUS building. At the top, viewed through floor to ceiling glass windows, is a beautiful panorama of the city, and I spent my time inside sitting on a bench by the elevator waiting for everyone to come back. When we were back on mother earth I wanted to kiss the ground. Another time I was in Toronto and refused to go up the CN tower for the same reason.

I am a little claustrophobic. When flying I prefer to sit in the aisle seat. First of all that means I don't have to look out the window, and secondly I'm not completely surrounded with no place to go. Phobias are actually fears or aversions magnified to the nth degree, and are very real to those of us who suffer from them.

Sometimes fear has a very real basis. I panic when my arms are held down and I can't move them. This is a result of the neighbor's boy holding my arms down while he was trying to molest me. Instantly my mind goes back to that situation, and I become that frightened little girl again.

Most of what we are afraid of exists only in our minds. We have catastrophic thinking; everything is blown out of proportion and we create mental pictures which, when compared to the facts, are extreme and usually invalid. Our mind focuses on a scenario of imminent disaster.

The hardest part about fear is determining what's real and what isn't. In 1957 the Russians launched the first satellite called Sputnik into space. This was the era of the cold war between Russia and the United States. Back then, people were encouraged to have well supplied bomb shelters in their back yards in case an atomic bomb was dropped on them. Looking back, this was foolishness, but then people believed this was possible. We must remember that only twelve years previously, World War II had ended when the atomic bombs were dropped on the island of Japan.

When Sputnik was launched, the whole world was afraid. What did this mean? What was the purpose of this thing flying around the earth? In the context of the time, this fear was very real. Today there are hundreds of satellites and a space station and who knows what else floating around in space, and we don't give them a second thought.

Fear leads to doubt, which in turn leads to a loss of self-confidence. When I had my business I had two main fears. The first was the fear of failing. If I didn't start, I couldn't fail. The second was the fear of success. What If I achieved what I was seeking, and then found out I wasn't worthy or good enough? What if people thought that I was a fake? What if I couldn't fulfill the expectations of those I was working with? What if, what if? Eventually I stopped trying and gladly sat on the side lines cheering and applauding those who were achieving what I so desperately wanted.

Fear is about not trusting yourself or anybody else. Fear is a lack of faith in our own abilities. Fear is not taking the opportunity to grow. Fear is paralyzing as well as demoralizing. Fear holds us back from receiving or asking for what is rightfully ours.

When faced with fear we need to ask ourselves one question. "When I look back over this time, what will hurt more - to have done something and failed, or not to have made any effort, and be left wondering what the result might have been?"

Overcoming fear is challenging ourselves to do the very thing we are afraid of. All we have to do is make one small effort. It doesn't matter whether we succeed or not, the sheer effort of trying forces fear to release its hold on us. If we can do something once, then we can do it again, and again, until it seems like second nature. Each time gets easier, and before long we are able to look back and wonder what we were afraid of in the first place.

TIP #26

SET UP A WIN

Much of our everyday world is governed by deadlines: arrive at work by nine, pay the bill by the fifteenth because if you are late you will have to pay interest, and so on. The result is that we live with a lot of unnecessary stress. Everywhere we turn, there is someone or something telling us what to do or when we have to have something done, arbitrarily, without any consideration to our circumstances ,or what is convenient for us.

Of course, to make order out of chaos there has to be start times and end times, schedules, rules, and regulations, but all this has done is develop a culture of fear. For example, a bill is due on the fifteenth but we don't get paid until the seventeenth. Almost immediately our mind goes to am I going to be charged a late fee? Will this affect my credit rating?

Recently I came across a similar situation in my writing. I write for the sheer joy of putting words on paper. I enjoy the rewriting and fine tuning that make my thoughts clear. When I am finished, I want to have the best possible manuscript in my hand before sending it to my editor.   My goal is very simple - finish to the best of my ability.

One day my coach asked me "when are you going to write the follow up to your book "Be Who You Be?" I told her it was nearly finished except for the typing. The end result of our discussion was that I would have three chapters typed by the time we talked again.

Suddenly, I wasn't having fun anymore. The typing

became work, not the natural extension toward my next step. I dislike the typing process, yet until I have a typed manuscript in my hand I'm not clear about my direction or focus. Sometimes I'm not clear about what I have said.

The rebel inside was shouting, "I will do this when I am darn good and ready, and not before."

On the other hand I was thinking, *"If I could teach myself to type each segment as it was written, then I wouldn't have this problem and end up being so stressed out."*

I should have been upfront and told her "this is not a priority to me right now because I am working on the second draft of another book, and I prefer to finish that first." This would have allowed me to work on my terms. Tomorrow, next week, I may decide to leave that project, work on another or type six chapters and think nothing about the effort I put in. I call this working on Judy time.

How many times have you done something because you felt obligated or don't want to hurt another's feelings? We complete the task, but there is no joy, and we often end up feeling a little resentful.

Now how different would you feel if you said to yourself, "I choose to do this project. When it is done I won't have to think about it anymore." Now you are doing it because you want to, not because you have to.

I strongly dislike the idea of goals. They terrify me because the very purpose of having a goal signifies the possibility of failure. I go through the process, put small achievable realistic goals in place, but all the time the stress is building. I feel this way even more if what I am striving to accomplish isn't of my own choosing, but somebody else's whom I am trying to please.

I need to understand the details. If I am going to spend my time trying to do something, first I have to know the why and how this relates to me. Basically I have to know what's in it for me. To me, the method of achieving is not important, as long the end result is the same. Your method and mine are probably completely different, but that doesn't make either of us wrong. Mine allows me to keep moving forward because I am working within the scope of my plan.

My Direct Sales Company held a challenge every year - add a given number of business associates to my team within a given period of time. For example, add three to receive a certain prize. During the time frame, I might talk to ten women of whom five express an interest. Out of these five there are three women who say yes, but at the very last possible moment one changes her mind. My final count is two.

Have I succeeded or have I failed? According to the terms and conditions of the challenge I have failed. On the other hand, if I made an all-out effort and have two new people for my team, I've actually succeeded. It's all a matter of perception.

Now, let's say my long term goal was to add five new business associates in the next four months. Now I have a good start and plenty of time to find the other three women.

Before I would have said, "I only added two after all of the work I did, so there's no possible way I can get three more to complete the challenge," then I would quit.

My fear of failing was so deeply embedded that I had

to find another way to focus on achieving. My motto now is "to do what I can, when I can, how I can, all the while keeping the end result in mind."

Maybe you are the opposite. You love deadlines and work best under pressure. You are at your best when trying to make something happen, success or failure isn't part of your vocabulary. This can easily translate into being so focused that you forget to enjoy your life. When there is no apparent deadline to strive for, you are at a loss. We each need to determine what works best for us, and then find a way to balance life with what we are working toward.

Sometimes in striving to achieve a goal we sacrifice our values. Then the situation becomes like a house of cards. We achieve the victory, but the foundation is pretty shaky. I have done this, and when the hoopla was all over, I was no better off than before. I was in way over my head and now had additional stress to cope with.

For me, the point is to do the best you can, to the best of your ability. Make your decision, knowing that whatever action you choose there will be consequences you will have to deal with. Have a plan or strategy, so that even in apparent defeat, you come out a winner.

Focus on real goals that are your own, those that will move you forward, and benefit the people you care about. At all times, we need to be aware that if we compromise our beliefs and values, we end up with a hollow victory. We won't feel the same sense of accomplishment and satisfaction. Been there, done that.

Failure comes when we either quit or don't try. Not achieving a goal may signify we learned one more way that didn't work, and now we can use this new knowledge as a building block for our next attempt.

Setting up a win means we regroup our resources, set a new deadline. and start over. The goal remains the same, only our method of getting there and the time frame change. A winner is a person who gets up one more time than they have been knocked down.

Tip # 27

TODAY WAS TOMORROW YESTERDAY

We can't move forward with one foot stuck in the past and one in the present. We may have deep conflicts, hurts, or guilt that we can't, or won't let go of, and then allow these traumas from our past define who we are today.

Compare this to lugging a big heavy suitcase behind you. It's so heavy you can barely move it one inch at a time. Every once in a while you stop, open the suitcase, take everything out with the intention of making it lighter. One by one you examine each article in the suitcase then decide you want to keep all of them. Everything goes back in; you reorganize, hoping it will be lighter this time, and start dragging it behind you again.

Up ahead are all of the plans, hopes and dreams that you have for your future, but that's all they are. You realize that at the rate you are going, you will never get there.

Now you see there are two choices open to you. The suitcase has to go with you, so you have to decide either to give up on what is in your future, or get rid of some of what you are clinging to from your past.

Either one is a difficult choice. We have been shaped by our past- all of the good, the bad and the ugly are melded into one. Everything is inter-connected.

Let's work on the assumption that you choose to move into the future, but it seems like an impossible task. If the truth be known, you don't even know where to start.

First of all stop and rest where you are. Today, right now, this very minute stop struggling and be in the now. Today is a special day, one you will never experience again. Take some time to appreciate everything around you, where you are, the people you are with, and all of the blessings you have been given.

When you are ready, open the suitcase, take everything out and examine the contents. First of all put back in your good experiences. Keep your victories, your accomplishments, your memories of people near and dear to your hearts – you get the idea. Now look at what's left. You already know not everything can go back in, so let's examine each one and decide what is still relevant or necessary today. If so why?

For example I am afraid of guns. I refuse to have them in the house. When I was a fourteen an incident happened to a school mate, who lived down the alley. His mother was in the hospital, his father was an alcoholic and was away from home, and he decided to play with his dad's rifle. One of the shots he fired accidently hit and killed a man working on the roof of his house a block over. The whole thing was an unfortunate accident.

For weeks I was afraid to walk past my bedroom window, in case there was somebody else out there playing with a gun. That fear is still in my suitcase.

I have to decide whether I want to hang onto this fearful feeling, or if I can still dislike guns, without having an emotional attachment. I decide my old fear of being shot at doesn't need to be part of who I am today.

There is no set amount of guilt, fear or conflict that you have to discard, one is enough for today. After you have finished, putting back in everything you have decided to keep there is still a pile on the floor you have to deal with. What do you do now?

Let's have a ceremony. Visualize a way of discarding these items permanently. Perhaps you can visualize putting them into a garbage can, locking the lid on, and throwing away the key. Maybe you can flush them. It's whatever works for you. A word of caution, do this in such a way that your actions produce a sense of finality. You don't want them creeping back into your suitcase taking up unnecessary room.

One time when I was driving across the Peace River Bridge I plucked my worries off my shoulder, opened the window and tossed them into the river. Another time I wrote a letter, lit the fire pit in the back yard and burned the pages. The wind carried the ashes up into the universe.

Sometimes we need professional help to deal with what's in our suitcase. We may feel ashamed or embarrassed when we consider this possibility, but know that it's ok. Think of it this way, the purpose of a professional is to help you deal with your situation, but in turn, you are helping them use the gifts and talents God gave them. They are helping ease your troubled mind; you are helping them put food on their table to feed their families. This looks like a win/win situation to me.

Some things will always be in the suitcase and that's fine. Your job is to tuck them into a corner, and not invest any more emotions on them.

I heard a wonderful quote the other day "you are not who your past says you are, but you are who you choose to be today." Our future is based upon moving that one foot out of the past and planting it firmly on the ground in front of us. Let's use our today's to their fullest benefit, so that when we get up each morning, we see that yesterday was a good day and tomorrow will be even better.

TIP #28

CLEAN OUT THE CLUTTER

I don't know about you, but every once in a while I feel the urge to go through my closet. I take out all of the clothes and shoes and lay them on the bed. My purpose is to weed out what I'm not wearing, then toss or donate them.

A few items go into the donate pile; one or two into the toss, everything else goes back into my closet. I tell myself they will fit when I lose weight, or maybe they will come back in style. Some I put back because I like them even though I haven't worn them in years.

I have expensive suits from fifteen years ago I can't seem to toss because each has a special meaning, and I don't feel a need to part with them. You probably know what I mean, and most likely have a few of these items sitting around yourself.

One day I focused on shoes; some didn't fit because my feet seemed bigger, some were worn out, and others had heels higher than I can wear now. I actually found a new pair I had never worn. Reluctantly I parted with my white heels because they were worn out, and the red heels which seemed too dramatic, the rest I stacked neatly back into the closet. They are there, when and if I need them.

Does any of this sound familiar? Even if the items were too small, old fashioned, worn out, not relevant or useful any more I hang onto them. Then, if I decide to buy something, like another pair of shoes, I look into my closet and usually decide I didn't need any more because I already have enough I'm not wearing.

We do the same things with our minds. The closet of our mind is filled with irrelevant ideas, perceptions, and experiences, thus leaving little room for anything new. Just as we need to de-clutter our closets, we need to de-clutter out our minds.

I would like you to make a list of what you believe about yourself. Write as fast as you can and as many things as you can in ten minutes, then stop. One by one look at your thoughts and perceptions, and examine them to see if they are real, unreal or of any value any more.

Some will be easy to get rid of, and you will laugh at your foolishness for hanging onto them. Some will be painful, possibly unbearable to look at. Some you hope to use again, some you keep just because. As you go over your list you may find that it continues to grow longer because you keep adding onto the bottom.

The first time you go through the list simply read what you have written. The next time you read through the list ask if what you have written is true or not.

Everything I need to do needs to be perfect	T
Children should be seen and not heard	T
I'm not allowed to have any fun	?
I would like to own a parrot	F
I deserve to be rejected by my family	F

Now go through your list very quickly putting a T if the statement is true, an F if false, and a question mark if you aren't sure. Some are easy. I don't like birds in a house so why would I want to own a parrot? That one gets crossed off my list because it was never true.

Now we need to deal with the ones that are left by asking ourselves is this really true or was it ever? Compare this to trying on a blouse – does it fit? Does it look good? Do you really want to keep this in your closet or could somebody get more use from it. You decide what to toss.

At a very early age I was taught "children should be seen and not heard." At five years old this was a very traumatic experience, but is it still true today? I have since learned I have a voice and have every intention of using it. Therefore this gets crossed off and put into the discard pile. No use keeping that thought in my head when I know it isn't true.

Getting through this list may take a long time. When we are finished, what we have left is what we believe about ourselves today. Notice that I said today, because this can change at any time.

Some of what we think has been passed down by our care givers, our situations, and our circumstances and are part of who we are, but that doesn't mean there is still a place in our mind for this type of thinking. Now we have a choice. Do we want to continue believing that about ourselves or not?

Back to our closet, once we have separated our clothing into piles we take a look, and then inevitably hang some back up. We aren't ready to let go yet. The same thing happens with our thoughts, some we decide to keep, and there is nothing wrong with that. Perhaps, at a later time we will re-examine that particular thought and decide we no longer believe it, and toss it away for good.

If you are like me, every once in a while you decide to go shopping for new clothes, and over time what I have hanging in my closet is more current and fashionable. I wear what's new; the older articles get relegated to the back of the closet.

Human nature abhors a vacuum, so when we let go of our previous thinking, the empty space fills with new thoughts and beliefs. We keep evolving, until one day we freely discard most of our previous thinking. Some of our ideas and thoughts that we keep are an integral part of who we are. They helped shape us into who we have become. Those we let sit there and exist. They are nothing, neither relevant nor irrelevant, and we have learned to accept and make peace with them.

I am a great advocate of writing things down. This act helps me empty my head of my thoughts and feelings, and allows me to release my pain on the paper. This is FMEO (for my eyes only). My experience, based upon the time I spent in counseling, has been that once I talked about something, opened the thought into the universe it lost its hold on me. Writing does the same thing for me and may work for you too.

When I was in therapy I learned a very important lesson. Some of the thoughts I had in my head, when exposed to the light of reality, weren't as important or relevant as I thought they were. In fact most of them weren't even true and never were.

There is a sense of freedom that comes with determining what is your truth is and what it isn't. Merely examining the thought or going through the process cleans out the clutter in your mind, leaving room for the new and wonderful things coming your way.

LEARN FROM HISTORY

This past winter Eva Olsson, a holocaust survivor, was invited to our community to speak to the school children about hate, bullying and intolerance. In the evening she spoke to a community gathering.

I was deeply touched by her message. She spoke for more than two hours to a completely silent room. We could feel her pain as she spoke of being routed from her home, travelling in a box car filled with people, and the random sorting of people at the Auschwitz concentration camp in Poland.

She told us of holding her niece while standing in the lineup, and a Jewish prisoner telling her three times to get rid of the child she was holding. As she got closer to the front of the line, she passed her niece to her mother. She and her sister were sent to the right - Life, and the rest of the family to the left - Death. Her entire family was gassed and cremated in the ovens that day. She and her sister were the only two survivors of their large family.

The women, sent to the right, were marched to a field, forced to strip off their clothes, and undergo an inspection by the guards. Anyone who had a mark of any sort on them, such as a birthmark or blemish, was sent back and gassed. Eva related that she had an appendix scar from surgery weeks before, but the guard failed to see it because of the way she held her clothing over her arm. From there they were completely shaved, deloused, tattooed, given prison garb, then sent to a lice infested barracks filled with women.

She continued telling her story of how she was

transferred from one work camp to another, each worse than the last. We could hear the fear in her voice when she spoke of the day the British and Canadians liberated their camp. Near death from Typhus and Dysentery, unable to move or care, and lying in her own squalor she was convinced she was going to be killed when one of the liberating soldiers marked her forehead with a red cross. Instead she was taken to a field hospital, transferred to a hospital in Denmark, and after many months, won her battle to live.

Jennie asked me why I related to her so deeply. If you believe in reincarnation maybe I was one of those condemned to die, and have come back seeking an answer? I had always been a little skeptical about how one man allowed, even encouraged, these barbaric acts to be perpetrated on other human beings because of their faith, but here in front of me was a woman who had lived the truth. Perhaps my feelings were a part of the deep sense of loss I shared with her when she spoke of losing her family. I'm not sure myself.

Eva and her sister had been raised in a very strict form of Judaism, and as a youth, she rebelled against the strict teachings. She was beaten by her father for wanting something better in her life.

After her release from the hospital she remained in Denmark, met her husband and eventually married outside of her faith. Eva and her sister both survived the horrors, but her sister disowned her for not following the teachings of their faith. Even to this day their relationship is strained.

I have read extensively and studied the Holocaust. I think I understand that those who survived chose to live in spite of all they were going through. They had a purpose, a reason, something to live for. They had hope, a belief and faith in a Higher Power.

Eva's message tells us we need to love everybody, not just those who love us and think we are wonderful. She stated that six million or more people died because a madman decided they weren't worthy to live; the sick, the mentally ill, the old, the very young, homosexuals, the maimed, the disfigured, the gypsy and the Jews.

Today wars are still being fought. Mass murder has taken place in Rwanda, Congo and Darfur because of religious differences or tribal affiliation. Today, in Afghanistan, the Taliban are attempting to impose their will upon the people. These wars claim to be fought in the name of religion but most can be traced back to intolerance. In Afghanistan the main targets are women, because the Taliban know that once women become educated they are a powerful unstoppable force for change.

To me, intolerance is about control, one side trying to force their will upon another. What doesn't enter into the equation is love and respect for us and for our fellow human beings.

Eva's message is one of unconditional love and acceptance. Let's face it; we are all kind of weird and wonderful at the same time. None of us are without fault, we all have our idiosyncrasies Inside we are all the same, we have lungs, a heart, blood, a liver and are all afflicted with the same diseases. Only our outsides are different.

Our parish priest, Father Raj explained that in India the children are taught their skin is darker because they live closer to the equator, and this helps protect them from the sun rays. Those of us that live further north have lighter skin so that we can use the sun's energy in our body. I wish the world would recognize that we are all the same no matter what color we are, what creed we believe in, or where we live. We have the same dreams, hopes and aspirations. I wish we could learn to be more accepting of those around of us, especially those we perceive to be different.

I firmly believe that every person has the seeds of good inside of them. Nobody is one hundred percent bad. The only difference between good and bad are the results of choices made during each person's journey.

We all seek attention in our own way. Those feeling insecure may be loud and bully people in order to be acknowledged. They may be the life of the party in order to hide how alone and frightened they feel. We often hide our true feelings or tears from those around us, ashamed that if they find out, they will think we are weak.

At some point we need to acknowledge who we are, what we stand for, and why we do what we do. When we finally admit who we are, we begin living on our own terms. We are free to be ourselves; the unique special person God wants us to be.

Part of Eva's message was that learning to love and be accepting who we are helps us become more tolerant of others trying to do the same. We are not perfect and never will be. As we work through the layers of who we are, we will come face to face with many things. It is human nature to focus on what we did wrong, or on how we could have done things differently. We rarely spend our time focusing on what we did right. What's done is done! We can't take back those angry words, hurt feelings or the pain we have caused others. Instead, we should focus on what we learned, so that next time we react in a different way. Instead of saying, I should have or could have; we can say to ourselves this is what I did, and what I learned from my experience. If we have hurt another with our words or actions we may need to ask for forgiveness.

We also need to make every effort to realize that we are good people who make mistakes. It is our birth right to be treated with respect and dignity, but first we need to learn to love and respect ourselves, accept who we are and the challenges we have faced.

After listening to Eva, I realized that changing the thinking of the world truly begins with our children and grandchildren. If we allow intolerance to fester at home or in school, they will grow up to be intolerant people. Six million people will have died for nothing.

TIP #30

EVERYBODY HURTS SOMETIMES

Looking back over my life I see the times of deepest learning and emotions were during my times of loss. Some affected me deeply, often right to the core of my being.

We endure the loss of so many things – death of a family member or friend, a job, a marriage, our health. We are traumatized, often barely able to function. We may blame ourselves. If only I had done this or that. I should have.............and so on.

To me, one of the most painful things to endure in the world is rejection. We all face this in some form at some time in our life; a child whose dad doesn't want him, a family who doesn't want their sibling, a customer who refuses to meet with you, a boss who promotes another less skilled over you, the child no one chooses to be on their team, or an NHL player released from his team without a reason. I could write a whole page about the different forms of rejection without touching race, color or creed. My good friend summed things up perfectly when she said, "There are all kinds of hurt in this world, and not all scars are visible."

How do we deal with this when we are the one being rejected? As adults we have a difficult time, what must a child think? I have little advice to offer except to try and realize this is only the opinion of another person, and that doesn't make it true.

In sales, I was taught that if a person told me no, I should mutter under my breath, "Go ahead and wrinkle.

Ten years from now you'll be sorry," then move on to the next.

In this scenario they weren't rejecting me personally, but were rejecting my suggestion, either because they weren't interested in my products, or I caught them at a bad time when I called. It might even be possible I interrupted a hot and heavy session of love making. Who knows? At a different time, and under different circumstances, I might have gotten a different response.

Sometimes though, the rejection is so deep and so personal that we never completely recover. This wound never completely heals, and any little reminder causes us to go back and dredge up our old hurt feelings.

This is where self-preservation comes in. The hurt may never completely go away, but we can learn to live with it. We can have peace of mind by making a choice. Am I going to let their rejection define who I am, or do I accept the situation as it is? Remember you are making this decision for yourself and for your own peace of mind. Each time we revisit the situation we are sub-consciously giving that person the power to hurt us again.

There is another side to rejection. We feel hurt because we are not loved, not wanted and so on. The person rejecting us has also made a choice - not to be a part of our lives as well. I tell myself that it's too bad, because they don't know what they are missing.

In my family situation, my siblings have missed our weddings, family occasions, camping trips, family reunions, anniversaries, birthdays - you get the idea. They don't know my amazing children or my awesome grandchildren. When I look at the situation from a different point of view, they have missed far more than I have. I got to spend those valuable times with the people I love.

Once again forgiveness is the answer. When we forgive, we do it for our own peace of mind, for ourselves. Basically we are giving ourselves permission to move on without that person in our life.

Sometimes we are the guilty party, and have rejected somebody. At the time the reason was important to us, but now we need to question if it is still valid today. Often people go through life having forgetting what their reason was in the first place. There is no need to become best friends, but it's never too late to say "I'm sorry." When we cause others deep emotional pain, we are also scarred in the process.

I am aware that if I ever reconciled with my family, I could participate in family functions, but I wouldn't completely trust them again. That would be too much for them to ask of me, or for me to ask of myself.

Why is it that we can feel profoundly sorrowful when we lose others or our possessions but we can lose ourselves, and not be aware that we are gone?

What's this all about you are asking? What is she talking about? Where is she going from here? I haven't gone any place, when I look I can see my hands and feet. I am here.

After this incident with my family, which I thought I was handling fairly well, small imperceptible changes slowly crept in. The opposite of rejection is acceptance. I needed validation, acceptance, and recognition that I mattered, that I was somebody. I needed people to love and want me. If my own brothers and sisters couldn't, and they were my family, then I had to prove to everyone else that I was worthy.

I became this other person, willing to do whatever I was asked. The word No wasn't part of my vocabulary. I found myself doing one hundred and ten per cent more than what was expected.

If I was asked to do something this meant I was being valued and recognized. The harder I tried to live up to other people's expectations, the more of a failure I felt I had become.

I don't know if you have ever felt the same way but it is a very frustrating place to be. Instead of being honest and upfront, I played my little games of self-sabotage. I would say "yes," and then never start a project which, of course, insured I never finished. As well as costing me financially, my self-esteem was taking a real hit.

I tried working with one Life Skills coach but ended up firing him. He was definitely not my type. Because of this experience, I found that when I began working with Jennie, I didn't trust her completely. Eventually, over time, I realized she was willing to work with me as I was; all I had to do was be honest with her. She had a tough job because my barriers were like one hundred foot high fences.

With her help, I was willing to ask myself the tough questions. Arriving at a certain place is only the start of the journey; the rest of the road is filled with pot holes, barricades and detours. All of these must be repaired so we can keep moving forward.

Do you feel that part of you is lost? Begin recovering some of these parts by being your own best friend. A good friend doesn't condemn, she accepts us as we are, which in turn makes us feel valued, accepted and loved. The golden rule is "do unto others as they would do unto you." I am going to change that rule to "do unto yourself as you would do unto others."

This essentially means treat yourself with love. Tell yourself the same things you would say to others. If you wouldn't say something to them, then why is it acceptable to say to yourself?

There is an REM video titled "Everybody hurts sometimes." Isn't this the truth? There are times we are filled with so much pain that we are incapable of knowing what to do next. If there is a light at the end of the tunnel we can't see it because someone turned off the power. There are other times we are so filled with joy that we wonder what we have done to be so blessed.

Once again, just when I thought I had everything figured out the ugly specter of cancer entered our lives. Evidently the time had come to learn one more lesson, and it's been a tough one.

On our first visit the Dr. told my husband there was a sixty percent chance that the mass he felt was cancerous. We clung to the forty percent chance that he was wrong.

Then the cryptic phone call that not only did he have cancer, but there was a possibility it might have already spread to other parts of his body. Telling the kids was the hard part. Dads are invincible. Now they were faced with the reality that their dad has a serious illness. That night, after they had gone home, my husband and I went to bed, but neither of us slept. I lay with my head by his shoulder; he held my hand against his breast. There were no words, just two people hurting, trying to give the other comfort and courage to face what was coming - something neither of us wanted to deal with.

In a perfect world, and on TV, the patient receives the diagnosis one day, more tests the next, treatment is determined next, and the whole thing is handled within a week. In our case, days and days of waiting were involved – book the tests, wait, have the test, wait for the results. This was the hard part.

The longer we waited, the more fearful I became, the higher my stress level became. I had to be strong. No one needed to see my cry, least of all my husband and kids. I felt like I was a bystander, completely frustrated with not being able to fix the problem. All I could do was pray and offer my support. Each of our children struggled with their own fears, and dealt with them in their own way. They were amazing.

As expected, the dam finally broke, and I became completely undone. It took several days for my thinking to clear before I realized I was letting my fear overwhelm my logic. Suddenly I began to understand that I could handle this one step at a time. That's all I had to do.

In our case the steps were have the tests done, get the results, next step decide on treatment, next step......... and so on. Rather than assuming the worst case scenario all I had to do was go to, then complete the next step. Waiting became more tolerable, and during the in-between periods we went about our normal routine. Well as normal as it could be, there was always the shadow hanging over us.

Each situation has a logical progression, so during the most trying times we only needed to travel as far as the next step. Concentrate on that, complete it. Go on to the next and so on. This helps prevent the projecting forward of the "what if" scenarios that scare the pants off us. The truth is we don't know what the future holds or what the outcome of any circumstance will be. If we could get up every morning and tell ourselves "I can handle whatever comes today," then that is all we have to do. Tomorrow is a new day and we will handle that when we get there.

This is one example of using your personal power, and looking after your own mental, emotional and spiritual needs. Once again you are in control of your own actions and reactions even though your world is completely upside down. Pray for strength and courage, and live with the assurance that you can handle the "next step."

I realize, that over time, even the darkest of situations will resolve themselves. I cling to my belief that God has a plan for each of our lives. How I wish I had understood that at forty rather than later.

Part of learning to look after ourselves is accepting that bad things happened in our lives. We can't dwell on them. We can't blame God or the world, all we can do is accept. We have to trust! We all hurt sometimes, but we can't allow this pain to consume us. Each of us has to find our own way to get past this moment. We can read the Bible, write a letter and let the pieces float on the wind. We could pray or see a professional. In the end we will learn to forgive.

We honor ourselves by living our lives in spite of the pain and the unknown. This experience is forever going to be part of who we are. We have to give ourselves time to heal, time to let the anger go, and time to come to terms with tragedy. We pay tribute to the pain by first accepting it, then moving on. Accepting our sorrow gives us permission to become who we are meant to be. You and I both know this isn't easy, but we do more damage to ourselves, and those around us, when we continue to hang onto the pain.

Each and every day, when we open our eyes, we have been given the gift of life for that day. We are charged with the duty to look after this gift. It is only by looking after ourselves that we are we able to share our gift with others. We accomplish this one step at a time, one day at a time.

TIP #31

BAD THINGS HAPPEN TO GOOD PEOPLE

Today my heart is troubled. This morning I heard of another young father in our community losing his battle with drugs. This is the fourth since the beginning of the year, another tragic loss. A son has lost his father, parents have lost their child and a brother is left without a brother. Our community, as a whole, has lost a volunteer, and someone who tried to make this a better place in spite of his own demons.

Bad things happen to good people. There is no rhyme or reason, but at some time we will lose something or someone we value, and are left wondering why. There may also be times we ask the question "will this ever end?" Will I ever be happy again?" It seems that the longer we live, the higher our losses become, and the more powerless we feel.

A very dear friend of mine is dealing with the loss of her marriage. After thirty five years they are fighting their way through a divorce. Love has turned to hate.

As I previously mentioned two of my friends survived the Slave Lake fire. One lost all of her earthly possessions, and was left with her car and the clothes on her back. To compound her sorrow, a month later she lost her husband to a form of Alzheimer's disease.

My other friend came through the incident with all of her worldly possessions intact. Visibly there are no signs of loss, but her security, her way life as she knew it, has unalterably changed. Again, within several months, she also lost a loved one – her mother. Things that seemed so important before the fire held little importance afterward.

A young man finally faces up to and begins to deal with the sexual abuse he was forced to endure as a youth. Now, as an adult, he must come to terms with the reprehensible act perpetrated upon him in order to live his life to the fullest. The sorrow each of my friends feel is unimaginable.

When I look over my own life and my losses, the most traumatic, until now, has been the rejection from my brothers and sisters. Why? I tell myself I am a good person, I didn't deserve this. No, none of us deserve the things that happen to us, but they happen anyway. The same for the previous examples, those people didn't deserve what they had to go through, but it happened and there wasn't a darn thing they could do about it.

When my father passed away I was eight months pregnant and having problems carrying my fourth child. I buried my grief, instead turning my attention to getting our baby to term and having a healthy child.

Within the next five years I lost my grandfather, grandmother, left my job at the hospital after eighteen years, and Bob lost his grandfather, uncle and father.

I held all of my pain inside, choosing not to deal with the losses; until the day came that I was overwhelmed. I tumbled into that deep dark pit known as depression. But, when I look back, I can see what a valuable and life changing experience that ended up being. I believe without that experience I wouldn't be the person I am today.

When my mom and brother passed I grieved openly, for each. I had prayed that God would relieve them of their pain. One day, about two weeks after my brother's funeral, I looked at his picture, and for a solid ten minutes yelled and screamed at him. Then I cried. I was mad at him for leaving me alone.

When all is said and done, we have no choice but to accept what life hands us, and find a way to cope and/or forgive. In order for us to move on we have to reach this point. To do otherwise is to remain stuck in the bitterness, anger and hurt. In time, those feelings will eventually consume us, leaving behind a former shadow of who we could have been.

When we are learning to look after ourselves we need to accept that bad things have happened to us. We can't change them; we merely learn to live with them. We accomplish little by lashing out or trying to even the score. Slowly I have come to the realization that whatever has happened must be a part of what was planned for me.

Grief is a funny thing. We mourn for the person or loss, but in reality we are mourning the "what could have been." We are looking at the rest of lives empty of what was, and will never be again.

Some losses are easier to accept than others. Some rock us to the deepest core of our being and leave us struggling to understand why. We have to give ourselves time to feel whatever emotions we are feeling. If we can't do this then we must find the courage to seek professional advice.

A few years ago a neighbor, who had just lost her father, came to me and asked, "How am I going to get through this?"

I replied to her "one day at a time. Eventually the morning will come when you wake up and don't hurt quite as much as the day before, and that is the day you will begin to move forward." We never forget, we merely adjust to our new reality

Grief, that deep sadness we feel, often rolls over us like ocean waves, when and where we least expect it. We hear a song on the radio, or pick up an object and suddenly we are sobbing. It's OK, go ahead and cry. You need to do this for you. Ignore those who say it's time to put this behind you and move on. So and so wouldn't want you to do this, or be this way. Their intentions are good, but be patient; the time will come when you feel ready to go on living. Until then, do the best you can, one day at a time.

Like I mentioned previously we can't allow our pain to overcome us. We begin stepping into our own power when we stand up and say "I accept that this has happened, but I refuse to allow it to rule the rest of my Life. That was the past, this is now.

The next thing to do is take action. Find a way to let go of the pain or humiliation you feel. Have a funeral; pour your heart and soul out onto a piece of paper then burn it or flush it, but find a way to let it go. This isn't as easy as it sounds, and there will be times when whatever happened will came back, but each time you dismiss the thought or idea, you are becoming stronger. We get to choose who and what sorrow we are willing to carry in our hearts.

One day during mass our Parish priest said "those we love don't leave us, they have only moved to a different address." We no longer have their physical bodies, but we still have the memories.

I am going to relate to you a true incident about the power of love despite loss. When my daughter and her husband separated I felt the loss personally. I liked her husband. He was always good to me and I was shaking my head trying to understand what was happening and why. One morning I cried out to my mother. "Mom, help me, tell me what to do. You went through this with some of you children, how do I help my daughter and grandchildren?"

The next day my daughter came over and said to me, "Mom, I had a dream last night about grandma. She came and whispered to me that everything was going to be all right." I burst in to tears.

She looked at me and apologized, "I'm sorry. I didn't mean to upset you."

I explained to her that the morning before I had pleaded with my mother for help. Mom had gone to the person who really needed her advice and comforted her. To me that was reassurance that she is still with us.

The bible tells us God doesn't give us anything we can't handle. Sometimes we want to cry out "enough already. I can't take any more," but it also says that He promises to provide us with the tools we need. Yes, bad things happen. We will never know why and perhaps we will never understand. All we can do is trust that this is a part of His bigger plan. This belief, this faith will help us through the rough spots and prepare us to welcome the sun shine of tomorrow.

Tip #32

WHOSE RESPONSIBILITY IS IT?

Jennie, my coach, forwarded an article to me by Dr. Jerry Overton called the "Victim Card." In this article he writes about the victim card being "like an emotional credit card in which we get a free pass from personal responsibility and accountability."

He talks about two types of people - those who play us and those who get played. I could see that there are times I have been in both positions. A victim asks "why me? Oh poor me. This is not my fault; I do what I do because............... 'You can put any excuse you want into the empty space. The other, I will call the helper, is always trying to fix things. The helper is trying to take responsibility for somebody else's life so they don't have to suffer.

As I continued reading the article a terrible truth dawned on me. I play both roles. When it comes to my siblings, I play the victim. After all I have been through, I feel I have earned that right. I want people to feel sorry for me.

More likely though, I play the role of helper. I buy into sad stories and apparent helplessness; I try to fight the battle for them. Each time I do this, each person I do this with, I am trying to convince myself that I am helping, that I am making a difference, but the reality is - I'm not. As long as I continue doing what I've been doing, I'm allowing the other person to continue playing their victim card with me.

When we are acting as the helper we tend to take the

responsibility and actions for others, and then if things don't work out, we are blamed. The whole situation becomes our fault thus allowing the victim card to be played again.

As a parent, one of the hardest lessons I had to learn was to step back, and let my kids make their own mistakes. Even harder was allowing them to find their own solutions. There have been times when I have had to force myself not to get involved, and place the responsibility where it belongs.

I have a friend whose son is addicted to drugs. He has borrowed thousands of dollars, sold their furniture, lied to them, and generally played havoc with the family. He uses the ploy is that he is going into rehab, so he can stay at home. In this case, he is the player; the parents are the ones being played.

When my friend was telling me her story, and without thinking I blurted out, "why haven't you changed the locks on the doors?"

"I don't know" she replied.

After reading this article I am beginning to understand some of the dynamics at work in these situations. The player of the victim card is the person in control. They have a way of convincing us to do for them what they don't want to do themselves. They resist any idea that forces them to be responsible for their own actions.

The helper, the one being played, doesn't want to put any pressure on them or add to their stress so they step in. They genuinely care for that person and don't want to be responsible for adding to their suffering. Each time I stepped in I didn't think I was doing anything wrong.

What I didn't understand was that I was doing exactly what was expected of me.

Each time we play the victim card we get something out of it. We may get attention or sympathy or whatever we are looking for. If our actions are successful, we stay where we are, continually repeating the same actions over and over. After all, if they worked once, they will work again. We want people to feel sorry for us. We gladly let them step in, and take the responsibility, and then whatever happens is not our fault.

God gave us the freedom of choice, and with that choice is the responsibility that goes along with it. For every action there is a reaction, and we have absolutely no way of knowing what the end result will be.

"One way to get control back is to understand that things don't happen to you, for you or against you. Things just happen. You are not here to control what happens. Your job is to control how you react to what happens, and the way you react determines how your life unfolds from that point on. The moment you begin to take control of your reactions you begin to take control your reality."

Coaching Compass June 21,2012

Therefore, as difficult as the idea is to accept, we are the caretakers of our reality. We are responsible for our thinking, and where we are today. Sucks doesn't it? Even reading and writing this makes me want to shout out that this must be wrong, but I know in my heart it's the truth.

It is important that we have the freedom to exercise our choices. Sometimes we fail to do this it is because the fear of the unknown is worse than our present situation.

The players of the victim card usually go through their entire life trying to make everyone else responsible for their problems, or always putting the blame on another for what is happening to them. I have seen many circumstances where, if the victim, ever once admitted they were wrong or were mistaken about one thing, their life would come crashing down. They would be forced to take a look and see how much of what has happened to them was actually their own fault.

The helper needs to learn to step back and realize that there is very little they can do. They can't make it better no matter how hard they try. Their advice goes unheeded, the money they give doesn't help, and they become extremely frustrated and possibly feeling used and abused.

So how do we turn this around? I learned one simple sentence that makes a powerful difference "what do you think you should do?" Someone has come to you wanting to be told what to do, and by turning the tables and asking this simple question, they are forced to come up with an answer. Once they tell you what they think they should do, they are responsible for the outcome.

The greatest gifts we can give others are responsibility and accountability. Accountability is doing what we say we will do; responsibility is accepting whatever the result is.

I guess the whole point of this tip is that we can't help people who don't want to be helped. Our role is to teach them to help themselves, and we do this best by stepping back and letting them find their own way. Even when they are struggling, we must let them continue to find the solution for themselves. In doing so, we are empowering them to be who they are meant to be.

TIP #33

FIX WHAT IS BROKEN

Like a bicycle wheel we roll along in our daily life, sometimes straight, and other times a little crooked. Over time our wheel begins to wobble because we have bent spokes, a few missing, and some that aren't seated properly. We haven't stopped and taken the time to thoroughly inspect the rim, the tires, and the frame and repair what's broken, and we won't until we are forced to. Eventually the wobble becomes so bad that we have no choice but to do something about it.

Life is much the same. Until we are forced to examine what we are doing, or what is happening, we keep going on our merry way ignoring the problems.

A few brave souls will now declare, "I'm fine. I have nothing that needs fixing."

I will pat them on the back and say, "good, I am very happy for you."

As for the rest of us, we probably have a few spokes that need repairing. Some we can fix ourselves, some we need professional help with. Some of our spokes have trivial scratches that don't affect our overall performance, others are damaged beyond repair, but we leave them in place because the surrounding structure is sound. When we look closer we see that some of our bent spokes are really the excuses we use to justify our actions.

We are unique, special, and a gift to those around us. We are loved, respected and wanted. There are those in our lives who think we are amazing, wonderful and powerful. There are others who wonder what spaceship beamed us down. We are survivors. We have taken what was handed to us, walked through the dark tunnel, and emerged into the light.

Even though two of us may have had an identical experience, we responded differently - according to what we know and what we have learned. There is no judge or jury who can condemn us for our response, because each of us deals with situations in our own way. Part of the learning process is learning to evaluate our responses, were we reactive or proactive?

Has reading this so far made you wonder what shape your spokes are in? Perhaps something leaped into your mind and won't go away so let's see what we can do about it. Once again I urge you to get your journal out. If you don't write in one, then find a piece of paper and a few minutes of quiet time.

First write down whatever popped into your mind. Often this will start with I wish....... followed by something we feel guilty about, something we did or didn't do, and has troubled us for a long time. "I wish I had told my dad how much I loved him the last time I saw him, because he died soon after. I wish I had taken steel guitar lessons instead of the violin, because now I play neither. I wish................" You get the idea.

These are regrets. They indicate choices we made, or others made for us at that particular time in our lives. We continue heaping blame upon ourselves. Peace begins to filter into our mind when we first acknowledge, and then begin to understand the reason we feel as we do, but sometimes we may be so broken that we need professional help. Don't be afraid! Don't be ashamed!

Never mind what others think. What is important is that you are looking after you. You are getting what is broken fixed so that your wheels will turn smoothly for the rest of your life. Also, be aware that we can't go back and change what happened, but we can to come to terms, deal with it, and move on.

Coming to terms with our situation is never easy. We have been hurt or damaged. We want someone to pay for what was done to us. We are angry, and want to get even. Other times we may feel overwhelmed with guilt over something we said or did. Our inappropriate words or actions have hurt or offended another, and we can't take them back. We are left in this quandary of what to do.

The magic word here is forgiveness. We do this for ourselves, not for or because of anyone else. Whether we have hurt or been hurt, we cannot continue to carry the burden any longer.

Out comes the trust old dictionary again. Forgiveness – "give up the wish to punish or get even with; pardon; not have hard feelings toward." I thought forgiving meant I had to accept what had been done or said to me, and I had to tell the other person that it was acceptable, and that I was no longer bothered.

Now I can say "what happened really hurt me. There is no excuse for what you did, but I'm not going to try and get even. I'm not going to hurt you back. I'm not going to let this bother me."

We are giving ourselves the power to move forward. What we are saying is, "I am giving up the idea of retaliation." We don't have to forget the incident, but now we can give up plotting ways to get even. We are giving ourselves the gift of freedom from the pain.

When we forgive, we are doing this for ourselves, for our own piece of mind and no other reason. Each time we revisit the incident, we unconsciously allow that person to hurt us over and over. When we can honestly say whatever happened has no consequences in our lives anymore, we are taking back our power.

Let's examine another ugly truth. Sometimes the other person isn't actually aware they are wrong because they don't know any different. The grandfather beats the grandmother and the son. The son beats his wife and children. His son beats his wife and the whole family is caught up in an endless circle of abuse. They are living what they have been taught. I'm not condoning these actions but I am saying some people honestly don't know that their actions are unacceptable to the rest of us.

I'm not saying we need to live with this unacceptable behavior, I am saying that plotting to get even does more harm than good. It's hard to fight ignorance; therefore we must look after ourselves when caught up in this process.

Remember that you are doing the forgiving for YOU. - to free your spirit and mind. I firmly believe in the saying "what goes around comes around." If this is true, then I only want good things coming my way.

In my family situation, I had to find a way to deal with the hurt and pain. I had done everything I could think of to change the outcome, but nothing helped. Eventually I wrote a letter to each of my brothers and sister's telling them I forgave them for their actions and the hurt they had caused me. I poured my heart and feelings into those letters. Then I lit the fire pit in the backyard and fed the pages into the flames, one sheet at a time. The ashes from the paper floated into the air, where they were carried away by the wind. Then, I handed the situation back to God to handle.

The hurt remains, but the acute pain is gone. I now accept this is the way it is, and go about my life no longer wishing for what probably will never be. I can and have moved on. I would be lying if I said this doesn't bother me anymore. There are definitely times when it does, but the pain is a brief ache because I know now there is nothing more I can do.

When we are deeply hurt, it's also important to allow ourselves time to heal. By travelling through the storm, we will eventually come back into the sunshine. Sometimes not facing up to or resolving conflict means we give it permission to keep haunting us.

During this time we also have to give ourselves permission to heal. If you broke your arm, the doctor would put a cast on it for six weeks, and then check to see how the healing was coming along. The cast gets in our way, but we tolerate the inconvenience because we know the arm needs to be immobile for the bones to knit and become strong again.

In theory this is what we need to do - to allow our heart to heal. Life will go on, but how we continue in our life depends on us. When we feel shattered, we need to allow ourselves as long as it takes for the healing to occur. Some things will take less time than others, but the procedure is the same.

Acknowledgement + Acceptance +Action = a person who cares about themselves –   essentially becoming the person God means them to be.

When we forgive, and when we accept, we give ourselves power over our own lives. We may never forget, but the hurt and confusion are gone.

Re-examine the spokes of your wheel, fix those that need to be fixed, straighten the bent ones as best you can, get help to replace the damaged ones, and if this is not possible, make sure the structure is strong enough to compensate. Doing this on a regular basis insures that your wheel remains strong enough to continue to carry you even if there is a tiny wobble.

TIP #34

WHAT WILL BE WILL BE

Years ago on the radio there was a song sung by Rosemary Clooney "Que sera sera, whatever will be will be, the futures not ours to see…….."

This morning I realize how true this is. Our best laid plans often seem to fall apart at the last minute. Everything turns out good in the end, but the path to getting there is completely different than what we anticipated. Other times, things turn out the way they were supposed to, and not what we had in mind at all.

For several months my husband and I were planning on going to a cousin's reunion on my dad's side. Everything was ready to go. The trailer was packed, all we had to do was grab the dog and go. At midnight, mere hours before we were to leave, I ended up rushing him to emergency with a suspected heart attack. Thankfully the problem was something less serious, but we ended up staying home.

"Is this the way it was supposed to go? Is it possible that we were meant to be here during this time?" I have no idea.

I try to believe things happen for a reason. The bible tells us God doesn't give us any more than we can handle, but sometimes he pushes us pretty hard to handle what he gives. We are forced to dig deeper, search harder, and push ourselves to the extreme limits of our endurance, and then just when we are convinced we can't handle any more, he throws us a lifeline. In the end, the situation works out the way it was supposed to. All of our worrying, fretting and stewing had no effect on the final outcome.

Our beliefs are always being tested. Recently my husband was diagnosed with prostate cancer, and to hear this was like being dropkicked in the stomach by both feet of a sumo wrestler. It was unfathomable, yet true. If God doesn't give us more than we can handle, then he just dropped a mountain in our laps. I'm certain he will be there to sustain us, one day at a time and one step at a time. Maybe this is what it is going to take for us to slow down, stop worrying and enjoy what time we have left together. I guess we'll wait and find out.

I have also found that there are times when we force the conclusion to go the way we want. This works for a while, but somehow it eventually unravels. Compare this to knitting a sweater, and you drop a stitch. By the time you notice, you have probably worked a few rows above that, and are forced to rip out what you have done back to that point of the dropped stitch, pick it up and continue on.

We could choose to ignore this dropped stitch and keep on going, but soon there will be a hole that gets longer and longer as it unravels itself. Now in order to fix it, we have to go even further back, than if we had fixed the problem when we first noticed it.

I hate it when these things happen. *"Why can't it work out the way I want for a change?" Why does everything have to be so hard, so complicated. Just once I wish things would go smoothly."* Does this sound familiar, or am I the only one who feels sorry for me like this?

I'm sure we all get frustrated at one time or another,

but have you ever noticed that when something is meant to be, all of the pieces neatly fall into place. When that happens I tell myself, "this is too easy" and am left wondering what is really going on and end up waiting for the one thing to come along that will make it harder.

Accepting the loss of someone who was young is very difficult. Why? What is the reason for this? He/she had so much to live for. We tell ourselves a parent should never outlive their children. For myself, I try to come to the conclusion that their work on earth was done early, and that they had already accomplished all that was planned for them.

I have no answer for this. An older person passes and we understand they have lived their life, but the young have so much ahead of them. There is little, if any consolation, in the knowledge that this was God's plan all along.

Some people go through life mad at God. How did he let this happen? Why me? What did I do to deserve this?

My dad was in his late forties when he had his first heart attack. Two years later he had his second, then his third. Fortunately, he was in the hospital, and the doctors and nurses were able to bring him back after his heart stopped. He was reluctant to talk openly about what he experienced. Today we know them as near death experiences.

After that, he was never afraid of dying. He told me about his experience; how he was floating on the ceiling watching the nurses and doctors work on him. He spoke of walking toward a bright light, seeing his family and his mother. She told him he had to go back, that this wasn't his time yet. He lived another ten years after that.

When I look back I see what was to be, was to be. He was meant to live the extra years. For sure, he didn't want to spend the rest of his life as a semi-invalid, but he was extremely grateful for the extra time he had been given.

One evening, late at night, he phoned me and scared the pants right off me. "Judy" he said, "three times your grandmother has come for me and I have been able to stay, but the next time I have to go with her. Look after things for me." To me he was talking nonsense, and I couldn't understand what he was telling me, but in less than a year he was gone. I believe now that was his way of preparing me for the fact that he would be leaving. I don't think he realized what a huge burden of responsibility he had placed on my shoulders.

It's never easy to lose a parent, but gradually I was able to accept the fact that this was the way it was supposed to be. This was God's plan for his life. While he was alive he once again became active in his church. Many evenings he sat until the church closed, basically babysitting the parishioners who were there. He became involved with the then fledgling Native Friendship Center in Edmonton. He lived to see many of his grand children born, and enjoyed his time with them.

This is part of the reason I developed my philosophy that our lives are pre-determined. We only have so many days, and how we live those days is governed by the choices we make. Our plans are His plans for us. Our dreams are His dreams, but it is our responsibility to for bring them to fruition.

TIP #35

SOME RULES ARE MADE TO BE BROKEN

My good old Funk and Wagnall states that rules are guidelines Society has put into place to maintain order. As I thought about this, I realized that we also impose certain rules to maintain order in our own lives. Some come from deep within our consciousness, and others are instilled into us from long ago. They may be archaic, no longer serving any purpose, but we still abide by them. Then, to make life really interesting we add a few more of our own. Here are some favorites of mine:

1. Children should be seen and not heard
2. Don't talk about sex
3. Practical is worth more than pretty
4. Worry about money
5. Always put others first
6. Don't ask for too much
7. Be honest
8. Better to be safe than sorry
9. Don't break the rules
10. Wear clean underwear every day.

The rules we use to govern our behavior are as individual as we are. Some, such as my rule seven, involve the ethical standards we choose to live by. Others are taught to us, and we blindly accept them as truth, even though they may be detrimental, and may be instrumental in holding us back from accomplishing what we want to do. The old saying (my rule number eight) "better to be safe than sorry" translates into don't take any risks, be careful, stay within your comfort zone.

I ask, you what is wrong with being sorry sometimes?

Sorry might add a new dimension to our life, add new friends, new experiences, new adventures, more challenges, and possibly be a life changing experience.

I live with the arbitrary rule "don't break the rules, if you do, you will end up in trouble." Trouble isn't defined, so anything that happens could be trouble, therefore trouble can be whatever I want it to be, thus proving my point.

Conflict erupts when we try to impose our rules upon another. We are all different, and throughout our lives we have learned how to govern ourselves according to our values. Everything we say or do is open to interpretation.

What to me may be an irrevocable rule may be of no consequence to you. For example I keep things. I hate to throw anything away because I may need it in the future. You differ in that you throw things away as soon as you are done with them.

You tell me to clean out the closet and throw away all of the junk. I refuse, because I may need some of the things in there again, and this results in conflict. I frustrate you because I won't do what you tell me, and I am saying to myself "just who does she think she is." Neither of us is wrong, we simply have different rules.

I realize this is a simple explanation, but we can easily project this forward, World wars erupt for the same reason - I believe this, you believe that, and both of us are convinced we are right.

Eventually we reach a point in our lives when we need to examine the rules we live by. Usually, this occurs in time of great stress. Is that particular rule necessary? Is it important? Is something we were told fifty years ago still relevant today? Are we even aware this is a guiding principle in our lives anymore?

As a child I was taught, "if you can't say nothing nice, don't say nothing at all" To me this means always be nice, don't hurt other people's feelings, and don't say anything you will be sorry for one day.

Sometimes, there is nothing I want more than to lash out and tell people what I think of their actions or remarks, but I say nothing. Why, because I may hurt their feelings. If I do speak up, and there is no logical reason why I can't, I feel guilty - not because of what I said or did, but because I broke the rule.

You, in the meantime were taught to say what is on your mind. I'm not going to follow this through, but can you see the difference? In reality, if I had said more and you said less, we would get along better than before.

Rule breaking involves risk taking – doesn't it? My point is if we continue doing what we have done, in the same way we always have, nothing changes. We will continue to get the same results. Some rules we have adopted have become comfortable habits, and it's important for us to be able to distinguish the difference.

Many of our self-imposed rules are neither necessary, nor are they productive. They keep us stuck. Risk is trying something new, and our learning comes through the attempt

I'm giving you permission to begin breaking rules that you no longer need. The less rigid we are governing our actions, the more we will experience in our life.

THE WOMAN IN THE GLASS

*When you get what you want in your struggle for self
And the world makes you queen for a day.
Just go to the mirror and look at yourself,
And see what that woman has to say.*

*For it isn't your husband or mother or father,
Whose judgment you must pass:
The woman whose verdict counts most in your life
Is the one staring back from the glass.*

*She's the woman to please, never mind all the rest,
For she is with you clear to the end,
And you have passed the most dangerous, difficult test
if the woman in the glass is your friend.*

*You may fool the world down the pathway of years.
And get pats on the back as you pass,
But your final reward will be heartaches and tears
if you cheated the woman in the glass.*

Author Unknown

TIP #37

LEARN THE LEARNING

My son phoned today frustrated as usual. His dream is to open a first class hair salon. Last year he moved from Calgary to Victoria, and since moving hasn't been able to find his niche or build a clientele. In Calgary he was active and busy, but moved because his partner's job transferred him to Victoria.

We talked about what his dreams and goals were. No wonder he was feeling frustrated. He has trained in London, New York and Las Vegas, and moved at the height of his career. I explained to him that it is necessary to get the learning, to understand what isn't working, and use this information in the future.

He started to tell me what he was learning, but I stopped him. I told him it was one thing to get the learning, but quite another to put it into action. He still has time to find his way, but as he draws closer to forty it is time to get serious about what he wants for his life and go for it.

We all do this. There is something we want, and we want it right now. We want everything in the universe to perfectly align itself so our dream falls into place. What we fail to recognize is that we need to take the necessary steps to make our dream happen. We need to understand what our experiences have taught us, and cry the tears. Instead of asking ourselves what are we doing wrong, we need to ask what we did right to get this result. We must learn to say, "If this isn't the result I wanted what can I do differently the next time I am in the same situation?"

Unfortunately the same situations keep presenting

themselves in different scenarios, until we finally learn what we are supposed to. I'm not sure that makes much sense, but if we keep doing what we have always done, we will keep getting what we always get. To get a different result, we have to do something different, and that becomes the learning. For some of us, this takes longer than others.

As we move through the process we become finely attuned to who or what we want. We take what God has given us, and work with these gifts to fulfill our purpose.

When I began working with Jennie, I had no intention of putting my learning into the written word. I wrote because that was my way of understanding what I was taking in. My natural learning style involves reading, hearing and writing. For me to truly comprehend something, I have to be able to see it on paper. My first book came as a direct result of wanting to share my learning with you. I rewrote the darn thing six times, until I was absolutely sure that every word was what I wanted to say. My sense of accomplishment came from holding my book in my hand. My dream had finally come true.

I couldn't have written the book without going through the process and learning the lessons, many of them over and over again. Learning to value my worth meant not seeing me as a Nobody and recognizing I am Somebody. The biggest lesson I had to learn was to get out of my own way.

I also realized that it is one thing to tell others how to live their lives and recognize who they were, but I had to follow my own advice. I realized I couldn't get away with talking the talk; I also had to walk the walk.

There is healing in this process – a letting go, an acceptance that what happened was only one small chapter in my life. That was then, this is now. As you progress through the process, you too will emerge a stronger person, and will have grown in ways you couldn't imagine were possible before. You have become a survivor.

Every ending leads to a new beginning. Eventually we learn the lessons we need to in order to move on. Remember also that these lessons are uniquely designed for each of us. They are part of the process which leads us to where we want to be, and to living a life filled with power and confidence. Our struggle may empower another, giving them the hope and the promise that, if we can overcome overwhelming odds, they can too. Your light gives them the power to light their own path, and, in turn, their light will empower others.

TIP #38

PROVIDE LEADERSHIP

Many times we have heard the expression "He/she is a born leader." Some people are born with the charisma that makes others want to be with them, and do what they are doing. President Obama with his, "yes we can," is a good example of this.

Far too often we think that this is what leadership is - being visible, being charismatic and standing out in a crowd, but it is actually something very different.

Leadership is about leading the way and taking others with you for your mutual benefit. Many a self-proclaimed leaders say "follow me" and begins marching down the path. At some point they turn around expecting a parade behind them, only to find they are alone.

To me, a true leader is one who says, "Come with me. I will go ahead to point out the direction, but if you become lost or confused call me, I will come back and we will work this out together."

For a short period of time I was involved with Welcome Wagon, an honorable company with good intentions. I had driven to Grande Prairie for training in order to become the representative in our area, and at lunch time the local representatives joined us. While we were eating, the leader stood up and displayed a gold bangle on her arm.

"You guys got this for me last year," meaning that it was a prestigious award from the company. "Well I want another one this year so get to work." Yes, she was serious.

I sat back and shook my head. Of course, there was the usual chant of "we will" and "we can do that." I have no idea what the end result was, because I didn't stick around long enough to find out. There was no way I was willing to put my time and effort into making her look good. Obviously, from this remark, all she was concerned about was what prize she would get, not how much effort her team would have to put in to achieve this for her. It was all about me, not we.

A true leader would have said, "Let's work toward your goals, because if you achieve your goals, the final result will be that we will all have been successful."

At one point in my Career, I had thirty six women on my team. I set the direction, established the program, but I let them choose their own way. Some were fully committed, some barely committed, and some decided to follow another path. Whichever path they chose was fine with me, because it was right for them.

At the same time I was taught to love people where they are at. They alone determine what is best for them at that specific time of their life. I could show them, encourage them, but until they could see what the personal benefits would be, I couldn't make them do anything they didn't want to. This was also an important life lesson. If you try to force people to do something they don't want to, you will never get the result you are looking for. In waiting for them to achieve what I wanted meant I was putting my fate into their hands.

Leadership is about believing in the leader. In 1992 Mary Kay spoke at our yearly Seminar about building the sales force to fifteen thousand from the then current eleven thousand. Her presentation wasn't about selling more cosmetics or making more money, it was about making a difference in the lives of other women. Her challenge was about connecting with women and encouraging them to become part of what we were so proud of.

Her incentive, if we reached the goal, was that she would return the next year. We did. She did, and that was her last visit to Canada. Shortly after that she had a stroke and lost her ability to speak. I remember how good I felt to be a part of this accomplishment. Along the way, the company was making more money. I was making more money, and she definitely was making more, but all of that came as a benefit of completing the challenge.

At some time we are all called to lead in some way or another. A leader is not a leader if nobody is with her. "People don't care how much we know, they will follow when they know how much we care." Leadership is about service, and is a responsibility to be undertaken seriously. Love others where they are at. Not everybody moves at the same speed, nor do they have the same goals and ambitions.

Recently I heard a leader remark "I run with the runners, those who show me that they want more." In a way I understand, and may even agree with her because that makes the job much easier, but at the back of the pack are many good loyal people who, with a little help and encouragement, are capable of great achievements. Those who are already achieving only need a little encouragement to continue. The people in the masses are the back bone of the group.

When we had our fuel business we loved to haul to oil rigs. They consumed vast quantities of fuel which was good for our production and our profits, but were a flash in the pan occurrence. They were here, and then they were gone. In the slow times, our regular customers were the people who kept us operating. They were there for the long haul, and we truly appreciated each and every one of them.

Have you ever sat and watched the heavens. Frequently a star will streak across the sky, produce a great show of brilliance and then disappear. When we look at the Milky Way, we see tens of thousands of stars join together to create a brilliant display and a lasting memory. True leadership is about gathering all of the stars in your Milky Way and saying, "come with me. Together we will light up the sky.

TIP #39

BOUNCE BACK ABILITY

In a newsletter I used to receive, there was a quote that read *"'the strength of a woman is determined by the size of the problem that stops her."*

This is utter nonsense as far as I am concerned. Do you agree with me when I say that we can usually handle the big things that happen to us, it's the little ones that cause the most trouble and pain? If our problem is big, we go on automatic pilot and do what we need to do.

Our little problems pile up, one on top of another, until we become overwhelmed. Then, one day, we reach the point of not knowing what to do anymore.

This is deeply magnified in a person who is a worrier. Worry is rooted in a small problem that expands into the realm of "what if" and then continues fanning the flames into fear. Most times this goes on inside our minds, and we remain blissfully unaware until it bubbles to the surface

Let's follow an example: the hours you work are cut from forty a week to thirty. Over a month this is a considerable loss of income, yet your financial obligations don't change. There are still the same vehicle payments, house payments, utilities and all of the necessities of life to be looked after. In the back of your mind you realize that the amount of income lost equals your car payment every month, and you need your car to get to work.

Merely thinking about not being able to make your car payment escalates to not being able to get to work every day, to losing your job. If you can't work you will lose your house. You and your family will be living on the street. By now worry is having a field day. Every thought leads to something worse than the thought before. This can go on until you become paralyzed with fear, and literally incapable of seeing what alternatives may be available. This is known as catastrophic thinking.

This information is coming courtesy of the world's greatest worrier (or so I am told). The truth is that most of what we worry about never happens.

A more logical process would be to take the time to analyze the problem from all angles and look for a solution. Your expenses aren't likely to change so you need to find a way to adjust them. Let's say, you go out for lunch every day which costs an average of ten dollars. What if, for three days a week, you took your lunch thus saving you one hundred and twenty dollars a month? If you like to read, you buy a library membership instead of purchasing two or three books every month. Suddenly, it is possible to see that with a few minor adjustments, you will still have the money for your payment.

A worrier fails to see that this new development has an upside. Now there is time to paint, or write, or spend more time with your family. Now there is time to do some of the things that never seem to get done such as washing walls. We can sit and wring our hands, or we can ask what can I do? The solutions are usually about money. Once we wrap our head around the idea, we often realize this is actually a blessing in disguise, especially if we are unhappy with our job.

The positive part of this exercise is that instead of giving fear free rein and allowing it to take over; we are meeting the challenge head on. We seek and find ways to make this situation work for our benefit, and bolster our ability to deal with a crisis.

So what do I mean by the title bounce back ability? Remember those red, white and blue rubber balls? When we bounced one on the floor it came back up. If we left it bouncing, each bounce would be shorter than the one before until it finally rolled to a stop. Also, with each bounce, the ball ended up in a different place.

Imagine with me that you are the ball and the height you drop from is actually a problem. On a scale of 1-10, your problem is a 12. On the first bounce the problem is still there, but when you hit the ground you gained a little perspective. On the next bounce you don't go quite so high, indicating the problem is becoming smaller. This action is repeated until the problem has no height; you bounce one or two more times then roll to a stop. That problem has been dealt with, on to the next.

Each time we go through this process, we gain confidence in our ability to make logical decisions and increase our knowledge, proving that we can overcome adversity if we tackle the problem head on. Those two little devils worry and fear, lose their ability to overwhelm us.

Sometimes we have so many balls bouncing we can't manage all of them at one time, then what? Some of these balls we can't do anything about, because they are out of our control so we let them do their thing. We choose the most important, and act upon them to the best of our ability.

There have been times when I have said "God, this is more than I can handle; therefore I am giving you this problem to look after." He will if you let Him. More often, we are reluctant to give our problems away because we want a say in the results. We give them to God, and if we think He isn't moving fast enough, we snatch them back. What we fail to realize is that He continues doing His own thing until our problem is resolved the way it is supposed to be. All of our tears, fears, worry and anxieties have no bearing on the solution.

I use my journal and daily writing to help me solve my problems. I write about how I am feeling, what my worry is, and why I am afraid, until eventually I begin writing solutions. I see a light at the end of the tunnel you might say.

Much of the time, our dilemmas are the result of putting off a decision. We know what we have to do, but we don't want to. We find a lump in our breast, yet we put off going to the doctor because we are afraid of the outcome. Finally we make the appointment, after convincing ourselves that we can deal with whatever is to come. The not knowing and the waiting are the worst parts. If you are like me, when you finally do make a decision, you feel relieved. We bounced the ball; now we can solve the problem, keeping in mind what is best for us.

Bounce back ability is being able to take that kick in the stomach, picking ourselves up, dusting ourselves off and keeping on. We place our trust in the fact that our problem will eventually work out the way it was supposed to.

TIP #40

FLEX- ABILITY

When I use the term flex-ability I don't mean physically being able to reach down and touch the floor with the palm of your hand. I mean how rigid are you in your thinking and attitudes? Are you willing to see another's point of view, or is your opinion the only one that counts?

I love the inspirational covers on Journal notebooks. Each presents a new opportunity to buy the book and fill the pages with words. Yet, when I get close to the end of one, I begin trying to figure out which one I will use next. I always seem to have four or five to choose from, so do I choose one that is pretty, or does it have to be one of the more practical unused scribblers that I saved from heaven knows when? After much dithering I decide on a pretty one, like we are talking about having made a major decision.

On the front of the book I am currently using it says there are ninety six pages, but before I get to the end, I am looking forward to writing in a new one. If the cover says there are ninety six pages, does this mean that I have to use every page, or can I leave the last few pages blank? My mind tells me if there are ninety six pages then I am supposed to use every one of them. What's the old adage "waste not, want not."

You can stop snickering any time. I was brought up with the understanding that rules were rules and you followed them. Practical ones such as "don't put your elbows on the table when you are eating, don't slurp your soup, don't run around the house without a housecoat on, don't walk in the house with your shoes on," have stayed with me all of my life. I'll bet if you think about the rules you follow, you could probably add a few more to the list. These subconscious rules keep us rigid in our thinking and our actions.

Flex-ability doesn't mean compromising our own morals and ethics. Rather, it means that because something has always been done in a certain way doesn't mean it always has to be done that way. We have to be willing to experiment with new thinking and new ideas, and try new things before we actually know what is best for us.

Earlier I used the illustration of paddling upstream against the current. The sheer effort is exhausting. If the current is strong enough, and no matter how hard we paddle, we end up going backwards.

Once again we have a choice. We want to go from Point A downstream to Point B. We can choose to battle the strong current going upstream until we eventually lose enough ground that we end up at Point B, or we can face forward, float with the current, and face the obstacles coming in our direction. Paddling upstream means we are always facing where we have come from, and frequently end up being blindsided by the obstacles that come along.

Don't get me wrong. There is a place for rules in our society, but being flexible, and adapting when and where necessary is much easier on us.

We can either fight change with everything we possess, or we can go with the changes making them work to our benefit. This means using our ethics and values to help us adapt to the new circumstances.

Flex-ability can bring new problems, new thoughts and new feelings. Sometimes the changes don't work the way we want them to, but we learn and keep pressing forward. There is a reason we walk in the valleys – we learn and grow. Then, when we reach the mountain tops we are able to celebrate our victories.

TIP #41

BECOME A VOLUNTEER

I was going through my files and found a newspaper article I had cut out of the Edmonton Journal, dated December 2000, which contained the following quote:

"You achieve real meaning and purpose when you feel you are serving."

Brian Tracy

Precisely what does this mean? Another word for serving is contribution, a person giving of themselves to do something useful for another. To volunteer is to be a part of something bigger than you, sharing your talents, gifts and abilities.

I hear some of you saying "don't lay that one on me. I barely have enough time for everything I need to do for myself, never mind doing for others. I'm busy making a living. Besides, what has anyone ever done for me?"

In return I ask you, how do you think organizations and communities function? They do so because people are willing to give their time and effort. They also have busy lives, but find time to give back what was so generously given to them. Some of my most endearing and valuable moments have occurred when I was volunteering.

Of course, there were times I resented the time I was giving, but the effort was worth it. Sometimes I got involved because of my children, other times because I wanted to. Sometimes the project interested me, and I wanted to be part of it. Other times the community benefited, and sometimes I was the only one to benefit.

I love the concept of learning. When September rolls around my kids let me buy a few school supplies for my grandchildren, because there is still a part of me that wishes I was going to school too. Because of this, I have been involved with the Adult Learning Council in our area for more than twenty nine years. The classes offered are fun, interactive, and teach new skills, but more importantly they allow people with a common interest to come together.

Years ago, the government developed the idea of Family and Community Services (FCSS). This interested me, so I volunteered to be on the steering committee for our town. Today, this Agency functions as an integral part of our community coordinating and offering valuable services.

Sadly the list of volunteers is getting smaller and older. The same people are doing most of the work. There is a rule known as the 80/20 rule that states eighty percent of the work is done by twenty percent of the people. When we give of ourselves, we create a sense of wellbeing within ourselves. We know we are making a difference, that our actions are benefiting others. Often the financial rewards are low, but the personal "feel good "is high.

Many of the most important functions in our community are staffed by volunteers. These are men and women who donate their time to fight the fire at your neighbor's house or attempt to save the community arena. They know they are putting their lives on the line every time they are called out, but willingly take the risk because they care.

There is the coach who volunteers his time to teach our children how play hockey, baseball, or soccer. There is the man who spends hours each spring being an umpire so the fastball game is played fairly. There is the stranger who mysteriously ploughs out your drive way after a big snow storm. Every one of these people add to our quality of life and expects little in return. They do this because they want to.

I hear you when you say "I tried coaching a minor hockey team once and never again. All I got was abuse from the parents. I'm done. I don't need people treating me that way. Their little Johnny can barely skate from one end of the ice to the other, and his parents act like he is the next Wayne Gretzky. I have to be fair to each player; every child deserves an opportunity to play."

I'll bet you have heard something like this at one time or another, especially if you are involved with sports. The fact is we take the games far too seriously. Remember these games are for the growth and development of children.

In almost every organization I have been involved with, there is conflict; one person keeps trying to impose their will upon the others until someone eventually quits. We need to learn to appreciate those who give their time and effort.

Volunteers can do amazing things. Several years ago the communities in our area were approached to help provide grass root funding for a cancer drug trial. The drug wasn't new; the pharmaceutical companies weren't interested because there was no patent to obtain and limited profits to be made. Drug trials are very expensive, and without financial backing this one could not proceed.

Most of us have been touched by cancer in one form or another. I lost my two grandmothers, my mother and my brother to this disease. We all know someone who has battled the disease, or is battling the disease themselves. Unfortunately, we all know too many who lost their fight.

A volunteer committee was struck in to raise funds for this treatment. Nobody knew for sure if the drug would work, but without the needed money, there would be no way to find out. This amazing group of volunteers raised over one hundred thousand dollars from our community alone. Nobody expected the overwhelming support they received. The volunteers took an idea and ran with it. Currently the drug is in trials, and is found to be effective against some types of cancer. If the drug becomes standard treatment, every person who played a part in the fundraising will have the satisfaction of knowing they helped make a difference and changed lives.

As we grow older time often hangs heavy on our hands. Some people isolate themselves because they no longer feel useful. Our community needs you. We need your time, your expertise, your knowledge and your talent. Getting involved will keep you active, your mind alert, but more importantly, you will feel appreciated. Whatever small amount of time you can give will add value to your life and to those around you.

The greatest gifts we can give are our time, our expertise and our talent. People serving people are what makes the world go around. Serving others benefits us personally, and we never know when we may be the one benefiting from the service of another. We must be willing to serve and do our part to make this a better community,

TIP #42

TIME WAITS FOR NO ONE

This past weekend we attended a family reunion on my husband's side. They try to get together every five years, and this year more than two hundred and fifty people attended. It's a large family, and other years there have been as many as four hundred attend.

What tugged at my heart was how many people we had lost since the previous reunion. I missed their loudness, sibling rivalry and their hi-jinx, but most of all I missed their presence.

Our favorite uncle was there, but he has been diagnosed with Alzheimer's since we saw him last year. My heart felt like it was breaking seeing this once vibrant man staring straight ahead with that vacant look in his eyes. I realized that when the next reunion rolls around, we will be the old ones, and most of the aunts and uncles will be gone.

Where has the time gone? It seems not that long ago I was rocking my babies, now they are grown up and I have rocked theirs. I guess life is consumed in the passage of time in which few of us really took the time to live.

One morning I woke up to the realization that other people see me as old. Just who do they think they are? I want to tell them, "*I'm not old. I have places to go, things to do, and people to meet yet. My mind wants to soar, and do everything right now.*" Reality is that I have lived most of my years and can't afford to put things off any longer."

What prompted these feelings? Words such as old age

pension, senior's discount and retired now apply to me. These words imply our usefulness has passed, and like a quart of milk, we are beyond our expiration date. Most people don't realize that the product is still good even if the expiry date has passed. The only difference may be a slight change in the quality of the product. These words imply that we have little, if anything left to offer, that we should sit back, and shrivel up like old prunes.

These words should imply freedom - freedom from raising a family and responsibility, freedom to sing and travel and enjoy our lives. We should be free to do what we want, when we want, and how we want on any given day.

We each receive the same twenty four hours in a day, one thousand four hundred and forty minutes. We can choose to use them wisely, or we can squander them. The thing is, we are only given so many of these time frames, and then they are gone.

The idea is to use our passage of time as well as we can, and let others do the same. Life is too short to be focused on money or fighting. In doing so, we lose those precious moments of serenity. We forget how to live. We fail to grasp the concept that our journey is a marathon, not a sprint.

There are times I yearn to go back to when I could wear my pink hot pants outfit to the bar or spend our summer holidays together as a family in a nearby gravel pit. The one thing I know for sure is that I was always too busy to enjoy the experience. Today, when a stinky crude oil truck passes them on the highway my children say, "Mom, remember when......" This smell takes them back to the good times we had living in a small wooden homemade trailer in a gravel pit with other families. We had no running water, no flush toilets, and spent our time riding back and forth in the gravel truck for something to do.

Many perfectly able people get old before their time. The number of years we carry is irrelevant. These people give up, lose interest in doing things or going places, and are waiting to die. There is a real sweetie living in town. She is ninety eight years, and can't resist patting a man on the bum when he gets close to her. She is still making the most of every day, and the old fellows don't seem to mind either.

Life is what we make it, but while we are deciding, time is passing us by. In a blink of an eye we seem to go from twenty to forty then sixty, and then wonder where the years went.

Erma Bombeck wrote her essay *If I had my life to Live Over* after she was diagnosed with terminal cancer. *"If I knew then what I know now, I would have burned the pink candle sculpted like a rose before it melted in storage."*

What she is saying is take time to enjoy what you have. Take time to have fun, laugh and burn you good candles every day. There is no use saving them for a special day, because every day we spend on this earth is special.

Tip #43

RESSURRECT FORGOTTEN DREAMS

A Dream is a wish your heart makes.

Annette Funicello

Last Friday night, while we were out for supper, Bob and I began fantasizing about what we would do if we won the fifty million dollar lottery that evening. We decided to give each of our children a million, set up trust funds for our grandchildren, buy a big fully equipped motorhome and drive across Canada. At this point we had spent less than ten million and no clue about what we could do with the rest. Our ideas got crazier and crazier, but, no matter how wild our thoughts were, we couldn't spend it all.

I have always wanted to be a writer. In grade four my teacher, Mr. Albrecht, would read my stories and encourage me to keep writing. Not long ago, hidden in a box in the laundry room, I found some of the stories I had written as a young teenager. Today I am a writer, no, better than that, I am an author. My long forgotten dream has come true.

As we grow older, we sometimes look back and remember our forgotten dreams and wonder what happened. How did we end up where we are? Can you remember what your dreams were? Somewhere, in a distant corner of your mind, your dream still lives. It's never too late to pull this dream out, dust it off, and see what you can do about making it come true.

My ex son-in-law is a very gifted artist, yet rarely draws. As a child, he was told he had to "get out and work for a living." Now that is what he does, but the world is a poorer place, because he doesn't share his talent. His dream was to become an artist, but he drives a bus.

Each one of us has been given a talent or a gift that only we can do, one that is instilled in our DNA. Usually this is one of the things we excel at. Many of us are aware of our talent, but for whatever reason, leave it untapped. We either haven't recognized what we have to offer, or we have chosen not to.

The husband of one of my former business associates dreamed of becoming a motivational speaker. Today he speaks worldwide, and is an amazing man to listen to. Another friend's husband has a beautiful voice and does an Elvis imitation which sounds better than the original.

Some of you may say I can't afford my dream. I have no extra money for courses and so on. Today we can receive a free education on the Internet. Some sites offer step by step instructions to a project as a way of enticing us to sign up for their course. My grandson is teaching himself how to draw from a website they use in school. I use the free stuff, which is usually enough to show me how to venture out of my own. There are also some relatively inexpensive courses offered on line by various Colleges and Universities. I found one of these sites and took seven writing courses of six weeks duration over two years. I don't have a degree, but I have certificates that prove I learned the basics.

God gave you this talent. He put the dream in your heart and He wants you to use it. I would love to sell a million books, and make lots of money like Danielle Steele or James Patterson, but in the meantime, my long forgotten dream came true the day I held my first book in my hand.

I encourage you to get in touch with your little boy or little girl dreams. That particular one my not come true, but a different version still has a chance. Hold onto your dreams. Don't let them go.

Dreams offer us hope, because without hope, we are lost. Another thing about opening your heart and revisiting your dream is that you will never know where your journey will lead you until you do. Grandma Moses started selling her paintings when she was ninety. Maybe now is the right time, the time you have been waiting for all of your life, not all of our dreams need to happen when we are young. Sometimes, if we wait until we are more mature, the experience becomes more meaningful because we have a deeper understanding of life.

When we dream there is neither success nor failure. Nothing is impossible. We can soar as high as we wish, and accomplish anything we put our mind to.

There is an awesome quote by Les Brown, "*Shoot for the moon, and even if you miss, you'll still land among the stars.*"

.

Tip #44

ADOPT AN ATTITUDE OF GRATITUDE

Once again, I'm looking out my dining room window onto the beauty of an early morning. The sun is shining through the trees, the light blue sky is filled with white puffy clouds, the air is clear of the smoke from the forest fires raging around us. I am experiencing a feeling of peace and tranquility.

I am thinking about my friends who are recovering from the Slave Lake fire. Dianne, a member of our writing group has lost everything, her home, her writings, and her pictures, all of her material possessions. My good friend Marlene was displaced from her home for two weeks. Their home and store miraculously survived, but their life has been forever changed.

Both of these women are grateful to be alive, as are the many others who escaped from the burning town. With fires raging on three sides, seven thousand people were evacuated without a fatality. The surrounding communities stepped in to clothe, feed and provide shelter for those who had no place to go.

It will take a long time for the trauma of this fire to leave the minds of the town residents. The faintest whiff of smoke will send them into a panic, but eventually all will realize that they are alive. They have survived. They can start over.

We have so much, but appreciate so little. We truly discover what we have when faced with losing everything we take for granted. I look around and see how blessed I am. I have four amazing children, four wonderful grandsons, a home that is paid for, and food in my cupboard. I live in a place where I don't hear gunshots every day. People know each other and stop to visit on the sidewalk, or we can safely answer the questions of a stranger. We have four seasons, each of which brings its own special beauty

I moan and groan about the pain from my arthritis until I see once healthy people barely able to walk. I moan about the high cost of fuel and food, but without the liquid black gold that flows from under our feet, we would be broke and hungry.

I have the freedom to worship in my church, and safely walk my streets in the evening. Nobody is going to hunt me down and kill me because my beliefs differ from his.

Water flows from my tap, and I can use as much as I want. This is very different from the women of the refugee camps in Darfur who face the possibility of being raped every time they walk to the well for water.

I have freedom of speech. I can say whatever I want. Although others may disagree, I won't be thrown into prison for expressing my views.

My life is good, but I rarely take the time to enjoy what I have. I don't take the time to "smell the roses" because I think I should be doing something else. Our minds, our bodies cry out, "stop enough," but we don't listen; instead we look to drugs and booze to heal ourselves.

Many years ago, when I was fighting my battle against depression, the very gifted Psychologist I was working with encouraged me to find a positive in every day and express my gratitude. At first I didn't see the value in this exercise. What did I have to be grateful for? My life was a mess, I was a mess. I was barely able to get through a day, never mind being grateful for the opportunity to live that day. I did as I was asked because I didn't want to let him down, and over time, began to see what he was trying to get me to understand.

He wanted me to see past my dark gloomy self-centered thoughts, and notice what else was out there. He wanted me to learn to appreciate and value the small things that give me joy. I began calling these glimpses of reality "little miracles." To me they were. They gave me hope that one day I would return to that world, and leave mine behind.

Did you know there are people who can't sit in silence? They can't slow down their thought processes, and this makes them feel uncomfortable and edgy. When we are completely silent, reality invades our minds. When we are not distracted by noise, we are able hear our heart beating and the breath moving in and out of our lungs. After several minutes, we often become so anxious we have to get up and resume our busy activity. We are afraid of silence. Why?

Often it is because we are afraid of where our thoughts will take us. The busyness and confusion of our daily lives serve as filters that allow us to keep running away from what is important and needs to be dealt with. Silence forces us to realize that we can't keep running, and at some point, have to face up to whatever is bothering us and deal with it. There can be no more ignoring the problem and using Band-Aid solutions to apply a patch.

Silence offers us a time to focus on solutions. It may provide clarity, or help us recognize the call to action.

Silence also provides us with an opportunity to recognize, and get in touch with the positive things in our lives. Silence puts us in touch with the special person that we are. Silence often offers a form of healing.

Each of us should try at least once a day to find the beauty surrounding us, and give thanks for what we have. We may have cause to feel sorry for ourselves, but if we look around, there are others far worse off than we are. If we look hard enough we can find something, even on our worst day, to appreciate and be thankful for.

It is the small moments in life that add the most value. We only have today, this hour, this minute to decide how we will spend our time. Let us be truly grateful for what we have, cherish the people we love, live in the now, and count the many blessings we receive along the way.

This world is a beautiful place, and we are here for such a short time. Our minutes are numbered. We need to live, love, laugh and enjoy our time. Our children won't remember the big fancy house or expensive car that was so very important to us, but they will remember the moments they were hugged, loved and cherished. Most of all, we can teach ourselves to live with an attitude of gratitude, and with the realization that many of our challenges are small compared to those who live in the world around us.

TIP #45

FOCUS FORWARD

I have a cartoon by my desk of an angel holding a box with a ribbon wrapped around it. The caption reads, "Yesterday is history, tomorrow is a mystery, that's why today is called the present."

One of the unfortunate realities of life is that bad things happen to good people. Nobody knows why, things just happens that way. It isn't because we did something wrong to cause them. They aren't our fault, and we shouldn't accept blame for these unfortunate circumstances we have no control over.

We all have been faced with situations in our lives that leave us asking unanswered questions. If I had stayed home would there have still been an accident? Would lives have been saved? What if I had told my parents, when I was a child that someone had tried to molest me, would my life have played out differently?

Most of us have a litany of experiences we look back on and wonder about, but the fact remains, what happened to us happened. We can't step into a time capsule and go back and do things differently. There is no do over in life, but we are given a second chance by learning to change the impact of these experiences.

The first thing we need to do is acknowledge that we are survivors. We have taken the worst that life can throw at us and made it through. Of course, we are changed by the experience, but we are alive. We get to see and appreciate the sun come up each morning.

Before I went into the hospital during my breakdown, I had enough pills in my purse to make a choice. Did I want to live or not? Do I take the pills so the pain will go away, or do I find a way to fight through the pain and hang on?

Now, when I look back, I see going through that ordeal played a big part in making me the person I am today. My life contains an extra something which helps me appreciate the life that God has given me. I am a better person today for having survived the experience.

My today really is a gift, so if you don't mind, I would like to share with you some of the things I have learned over the past few years:

I learned I can survive rejection, and still have a good life. I survived my deepest fears.

I learned I don't have to accept being bullied or treated disrespectfully,

I learned that I have a choice, and the right to make that choice.

I learned to listen to my inner yearnings and desires, that it's not too late, nor am I too old to let my dreams come true.

I learned to never give up, for there is always hope for a better tomorrow.

I learned that I need to love and respect myself first, before I can do the same for others.

I learned that to forgive allows me to move on.

I learned that change is inevitable, so I might as well go with the flow.

I learned change can open the door to new possibilities I may not have seen otherwise.

I learned new and wonderful things are waiting to come my way, if and when I open my mind to them.

I learned I am a good person, deserving love and praise.

I learned that the lesson will keep repeating itself, until I get the message

I learned God doesn't make "Nobody's" He only makes "Somebody's." and I am "Somebody."

I learned that I had to let go of the past, in order to claim my future.

I learned life is a journey; each of us has to take on our own.

I learned I still have more to learn.

Each new joy, new sorrow, every year, every decade, every experience is an opportunity for us to become who we are meant to be. I believe God has plans for our lives, and the best thing we can do is hang on and enjoy the ride.

TIP #46

Life is an opportunity,
benefit from it.

Life is beauty,
admire it.

Life is a dream,
realize it.

Life is a challenge,
meet it.

Life is a duty,
complete it.

Life is a game,
play it.

Life is a promise,
fulfill it.

Life is sorrow,
overcome it.

Life is a song,
sing it.

Mother Theresa
http:/love-prayers-blogspot.com

.

227

Tip #47

LET YOUR LIGHT SHINE FOR ALL TO SEE

"A person living in their personal power has an inner awareness that makes them feel in control of their lives. They have a calm conviction about who they are, why they are and the ability to get what they want in life. They have a quiet confidence that they can set and follow the direction of their lives. They are able to distinguish the circumstances they can control and those they do not. They define themselves from the inside out. Using our personal power we can move mountains."

CoachingCompass.com
Feb.12, 2011 Newsletter

The previous tip, the beautiful poem written by Mother Theresa, pretty well sums up how we can live our lives making the most of every day. Our actual days on earth are few, and yet many will pass with their promise unfilled.

Allow me to digress a bit. In my sales leadership position, I taught my team members the 4 P's -potential, purpose, positive and passion. In other words, finding what they want to do, what expresses who they are and what fills their lives with the 4 P'S.

I brought many people into my business that had everything going for them. They had potential – the possibility of being very successful. I could see this in them. I wanted success for them, but for their own reasons, they didn't fulfill my estimate of their potential. Even though I wanted them to succeed, they had to recognize the possibilities themselves. Often I was sad, but never disappointed, when I saw them give up too easily. Yet I watched some of these same women go into a different direct selling company and do amazing things. I realized the new company or opportunity better suited the purpose they had for their lives.

Our purpose or **WHY** we do what we do often shows up in the vocation we choose. A chef's purpose may be providing good food for people to eat; a policeman's to protect others, a doctor or a nurse to help others. Very few people set out with the sole purpose of making lots of money. That is usually one of the benefits that comes from doing what they love.

Each person's **Why** is personal. The power of our purpose comes when we feel we are making a difference. There is always a reason that follows the why, and that becomes their purpose. I am doing such and such because......... Sometimes we don't even need a good reason to do what we are doing.

"I coach minor hockey because I feel that every child should have an equal opportunity to play. I wasn't a very good hockey player, but I loved the game. I showed up for every game, and it hurt to sit on the bench and barely have a chance to play." To this person fairness is important. His/her purpose is to see that each child is treated fairly.

Because I've felt disempowered most of my life, I feel my purpose is to help empower other women. I want to show my daughters, and every other woman, that they need to look after themselves, because if they don't, nobody will do it for them. I want them to know, that as women they are special, unique and one of God's most powerful creations.

Is there anything you are passionate about? Some are passionate about making love. They put their whole being into that special moment. Others say, "what again? Wasn't that one time last year enough?"

We can live our lives with passion. The painter feels this as she puts color on a blank canvas. The writer feels this as words fill the page. They are totally involved with what they are doing, time has no meaning. Their passion comes from living up to their potential and living with a purpose. They are living within their own Personal Power.

In her poem "Our Deepest Fear" from her book "*A Return to Love*," Marianne Williamson states:

"Our deepest fear is not that we are inadequate. Our deepest fear is that we are powerful beyond measure. It is our light, not our darkness that frightens us."

Powerless people feel helpless, negative, inert, and fearful, often feeling that their circumstances are beyond their control.

There is one more P we haven't talked about - Positive. Each of us has a choice about how we will react to any given situation. Let's say your boss is having a bad day, and she seems to be taking this out on you. You can react by thinking, "oops she is having a bad day. I had better keep myself busy until she gets over this," or you could react by thinking "who does she think she is. Just because she is having a bad day doesn't give her the right to take it out on me."

"Oh my gosh, that kid is in the mud puddle again, If I have told him once, I have told him a thousand times to stay out of there. I am sick of him changing clothes three times a day. Doesn't he know I have better things to do than clean up behind him?" OR "There's little Johnny playing in that big mud puddle again. I have asked him a dozen times not to, but he seems drawn to being in there. I remember being the same when I was his age."

Nothing has changed. The boss is still upset, little Johnny is still playing in the mud puddle when he knows better, but can you see the difference in how you feel? One reaction leaves you feeling upset and angry. The other gives you a measure of control over the situation because you chose not to let it affect you.

None of us are positive all the time. I like to think that I am a positive person, but even I have been known to slip into negativity at one time or another. Once we are aware, we can choose to change our reaction.

Recently I said to my coach, *"I feel like I am sitting on the lid of a box, trying to keep whatever is in there inside, but it doesn't want to stay"*. Another time I wrote in my journal, *"I am like a butterfly that has emerged from the cocoon and afraid to try my wings"*.

After a great deal of pondering, I realized the thing in the box waiting to get out was my personal power. All I have worked for, the pain, the grief, the realization, and the acceptance have been fulfilled. My journey through fear has passed, and I am at the jumping off point, ready to take the final steps of who God wants me to be, yet, I hesitate. Why?

It takes courage to step into our power because we are letting go of our excuses, and stepping out of our Comfort Zone. We are unsure where this new journey will take us. There may be times we aren't even sure if we like this new person we have become.

So back to the thing hiding in the box, despite my best efforts it will get out. That thing is my authenticity, the person I have learned to honor, and who I am meant to be.

As you step into your personal power and live real and authentically, others will see you differently. They will see you as happier, more content and more fulfilled, living your life with a purpose. When they see this, they will want what you have. You will become their shining example, the person they want to emulate

Once again, quoting Marianne Williamson, *"When we let our light shine, we unconsciously give others permission to do the same. As we are liberated from our fears our presence automatically liberates others."*

A WORK IN PROGRESS

We are a work in progress! Every day we are faced with the same challenges in a new form, and continue the process of evolving as human beings. If the truth be known, God isn't finished with us yet. There is still more to learn and things He wants us to do.

I became very discouraged while working on this manuscript. At first, I tried to write in the same manner as my first book. A light bulb moment arrived when I realized I couldn't because I'm not that person any more. I have healed, accepted and forgave what was necessary. I have moved forward, and to return to my previous way of thinking would be a step backward.

Now I had a different problem. What direction was I going to take? Every time I sat down to write, I was on a different path. There was so much I wanted to share that I was finding it hard to get started. *What did I want? What tools or tips could I pass on to you? Was there any value in what I was doing?*

In the end, I chose to go back to my purpose which, I believe, is empowering women. As grandiose as this may seem, I feel this is the purpose God has given me. If I feel and think as I do, and have experienced what I have, there must be other women in a similar situation. The way my first book was accepted by others told me that I wasn't alone in my thinking or how I felt. Hopefully, a few more words of encouragement will make a difference.

All I can basically share with you is that each of us needs to affirm, and then follow through on what we think is best for us. God gave us a mind to work with. He gave us the power of choice. He gave us the abilities to love and nurture. He gave us the strength to bring new life into the world. We need to use the powerful gifts God has given us as our strengths, but first we need to care about ourselves, before we can carry out the responsibility He has given us of uplifting others.

I believe women are the more powerful of the two sexes. Men worry that we will enforce our will upon them. My husband tells me the only place the man is the boss is in the coffee shop, the rest of the time they are only a part of the decision making.

My whole experience, my purpose for working so hard the last five years has been to get away from that feeling of powerlessness, and learn how to do what is affirming for me. Your life, your experiences also serve a purpose, and because they are uniquely yours, you learn in our own way.

If you are an abused women or man in any form, you already know in your heart what is best for you. I can't tell you what to do. The simple fact of knowing means that now you have a choice. The fact that you have a choice means you can consider what is best for you. Knowing that your life can be different, might help you to make the decisions you have been putting off for so long.

God gave us the ability to think for ourselves. We can choose to stay or we can choose to leave an alcohol or drug addicted mate, the debt ridden home, to be alone or tied to our job. We get to choose what is best for us and for the people we love and care about.

Ours is a quiet journey. Learning to love, nurture, and respect ourselves is a process. Once we have embarked upon this journey we are forever changed. Our journey doesn't end until that moment we take our final breath. I encourage you not to be afraid along the way. There may be periods of doubt, fear, and grief, but each time you act, you are becoming the person God visualized at your birth.

You deserve, no, you have the right to be who you are, but you are the only person who can provide the guts and determination to do what is necessary to work through the process. The message I want to leave with you is to remember that you are unique, you are special, and there will only ever be one of you. Let your light shine!

Others admire and love you for who you are. Continue your journey on a daily basis filled with determination to become all you are meant to be. At the end of our days, all we want to hear are the words, "well done, my good and faithful servant."

I have enjoyed sharing my thoughts with you, and this has truly been a labor of love. Each day I will continue to follow my own advice. Thank you for being my reason, for caring enough to allow me to share my journey. You are why I work so hard to fulfill my purpose. Continue filling your own well from the stream of life. Let your example encourage and empower others. Until we meet again, continue living your life to the fullest

About the Author

Known to her friends as Judy, the author recently retired from the business world to pursue her passion for writing. She lives in Grimshaw Ab. with her husband Bob, four children, their grandchildren and their dog Miss Tzu.

You can contact Judy at jcoates@telusplanet.net

15040164R00131

Made in the USA
Charleston, SC
14 October 2012